FRANK HART

The First Black Ultrarunning Star

FRANK HART

The First Black Ultrarunning Star

Davy Crockett

Utah Ultras LLC

Contents

I never thought of anything, least of all my color, only wanting to walk.

      – Frank Hart after his first running competition

Introduction

In 1879, just twelve years after the Civil War ended, Frank Hart of Boston, Massachusetts, became the first black running superstar in history, and the most famous black athlete in America. In a sense, he was the Jackie Robinson of the sport of ultrarunning in the 19th century, overcoming racial barriers to compete at the highest level in the world, in the extremely popular spectator sport of ultrarunning/pedestrianism (very long-distance running and walking).

Frank Hart's full story has never been told before. It is an important story to understand, both for the amazing early inclusiveness of the sport, and to understand the cruel racist challenges he and others faced as they tried to compete with fairness and earn the respect of thousands. He was the first black ultrarunner to compete and win against whites in high-profile, mega-mile races.

This biography also presents twenty-three years (1879-1902) of the amazing pedestrian era history as experienced by Hart when ultradistance running was the most popular spectator sport in the country. He competed in at least 110 ultras, including eleven in Madison Square Garden, where he set a world record, running 565 miles in six days in front of tens of thousands of spectators and wagerers. During his running career, he won the equivalent of $3.5 million in today's value.

NOTE: This tale must be viewed through the historic lens of nearly 150 years in the past. It will present news article quotes using the words and labels used in that era, that today are now universally viewed as racist, heartless, and offensive. But by stepping back in time, one can appreciate the courage and determination that Frank Hart experienced in a world that at times tried to work against him. Items in quotations are taken directly from newspaper articles of the era.

CHAPTER ONE

The First Black Ultrarunning Star

Frank H. Hart (1856-1908) was believed to be born in Haiti in 1856. He said his given name was **Fred E. Hichborn** although on several legal documents in the years before he started running, and throughout his life, he stated his name was Frank Hart. Once he became famous, some

claimed that he was from Columbus, Georgia, or Cleveland, Ohio, but throughout his lifetime, he consistently stated that he was born in the Caribbean, in Haiti, the West Indies, or Key West, Florida, and it was clear that he had not been born a slave. His parents were either William and Catharine or Joseph Hart and Elizabeth Mallory. He stated different parents at times and perhaps he was adopted by the Harts. "Frank Hart" was not just a stage name.

Adult school, West End Boston

Hart's family had means and immigrated to the west end of Boston, Massachusetts in 1866, after the Civil War ended, while Hart was a boy of about ten years. Why Boston? Haiti had been experiencing political turmoil and revolts for several years. The West End of Boston at that time was one of the few areas of the country where blacks were allowed to have a political voice. In the years following the civil war, many blacks from the South migrated to Boston. More than 60% of Boston's black population lived in the West End. It would be the future home of the Museum of African American History. As a young man in Boston, during the 1870s,

1

Hart worked as a grocery clerk and "general jobbing," developed into a talented athlete, and became an American citizen in 1878. He competed as an amateur in single sculling rowing competitions at Silver Lake in Tewksbury, Massachusetts, where he demonstrated "remarkable staying qualities as an oarsman."

Introduction to Pedestrianism

The sport referred to as "Pedestrianism" (long-distance walking or running) came into the American public eye as **Edward Payson Weston** (1839-1929) of Providence, Rhode Island, made several attempts in 1874 to try to walk 500 miles in six days. **P. T. Barnum** (1810-1891), of circus fame, had the brilliant idea to move such attempts indoors for huge audiences to watch, in his massive Hippodrome in New York City. In 1875, Barnum put on the first six-day race in history, won by Weston with 431 miles. In these races, the winner was the athlete who reached the furthest distance within six days.

By 1878, this unique indoor spectator reality show exploded in popularity in America and also spread to England. By the time Hart became involved in the sport in 1879, more than sixty-five such races had been held involving at least 350 starters, both men and women of many nationalities and races, and even a few black men. Black pedestrians were mentioned in the newspapers as early as 1869. That year, **George K. Washington**, of New Orleans, attempted to walk for 150 hours in a Hartford, Connecticut Hall.

Many amateur walkers and runners wanted to break into the sport to achieve both fame and immense fortune in winnings and wagers. In 1878 the British introduced race rules called, "go-as-you-please" which allowed running in addition to walking, helping the Brits to catch up to the Americans who had been dominating the ultra-distance strict heel-toe walking sport.

Pedestrianism also became popular in black communities. In April 1876, **John Briscow** called "the colored pedestrian" attempted a 50-hour walk without sleep or rest in a billiard saloon, in Washinton D.C. He swelled up and had to quit six hours short. In March 1879, a 25-hour race was conducted in Baltimore, Maryland, for all the "colored pedestrians" in the area. Black pedestrians competing against whites was still a rare occurrence.

Hart Enters the Sport, Crossing the Racial Barrier

Hart married at age 19, on September 23, 1875, in Boston to **Mary Augusta Berry** (1855-1898), who had been born in Norfolk, Virginia. He was working as a teamster at the time of his marriage, gave Key West, Florida as his birthplace on the marriage record, used the surname of Hart rather than Hichborn, and bumped his age up a year to 20, which was common.

Marriage Record, 1875 Massachusetts State Vital Records

The Harts had two children and lived in the black section of Boston near Cambridge Street in Boston's West End. Their son, **Francis "Frank" S. Hart** was born on April 14, 1876. They were living at 21 N. Grove St. Frank gave his name as "Francis" on the birth record, stating he was born in Haiti, and his occupation was a fireman. Their daughter, Sarah Maynard Hart (1878-1880) was born April 27, 1878, at 6 Strong Place, just

Cambridge Street, Boston

south of Cambridge Street. Hart listed the West Indies as his birthplace in her birth record and stated that he was a laborer.

In 1879, Hart jumped into the pedestrian sport with only a little serious training in a quest to earn more money. He said, "I don't really know how I became a pedestrian. I think I caught the infection in the air, like some others. I heard a good deal about walking and when I came to try, I found I could walk too. So, liking it, I kept on it and continued to exercise. I found it did not fatigue me and I went right ahead but knew nothing about training myself or what was necessary to preserve my condition."

BOSTON MUSIC HALL.

FRIDAY, SATURDAY, April 25, 26.
The Sporting Event of the Year!
A GRAND RACE!
THIRTY HOURS'
"GO-AS-YOU-PLEASE."
OPEN TO ALL.
Entries closed April 22, with over thirty of the best runners and walkers in New England.
Prizes, Gold Medal and Purse $175. Medal and $100 to first and $50 to second and $25 to third.
Military Band. Admission 25 Cents.
Doors open FRIDAY, April 25, 5.30 P. M. Race starts 6 P. M., sharp.

Hart did have some help and was "thoroughly drilled, trained, and tested to the satisfaction of those interested" before he entered his first race. His first race was held on April 25-26, 1879. It was a 30-hour go-as-you-please (running or walking permitted) competition held at the Music Hall in Boston, with a prize of $100 going to the winner. The race was open to all and was put on by **Fred J. Englehardt** of Boston, the editor of *Frank Leslie's Sporting Times*. The local sportsmen wanted to find runners to represent the state in an upcoming multi-state long-distance running competition.

Englehardt did not know Hart was a black man until he saw him at the start. When Englehardt announced the starters, some of the other competitors objected to having a black man run in the race. Englehardt told them that Hart would run and if they did not like it, they could get out of the race. They all ran. Despite opposition, Hart and Englehardt can be credited for breaking the 19th-century color barrier in ultrarunning.

Englehardt made sure that neither race nor ethnicity would be a barrier in this historic ultra. "The large field included a colored aspirant, several Irishmen, an Indian, an Englishman, and several Yankees." Hart said, "I never thought of anything, least of all my color, only wanting to walk." He knew that he needed to win, or he would be back to selling groceries.

The Go-as-You-Please Race at Music Hall.

Hichborn Looked Upon as a Sure Winner.

Forty men started at 6 p.m. on April 25, 1879. Hart certainly was not among the betting favorites, rather he was a curiosity, along with the "Canadian half-breed Indian," Tayaguariel. The spectators were surprised when "the Indian" took the lead followed by Hart, who kept his eye on the leader and eventually passed him into the lead after about six hours and thirty-one miles. Some competitors and spectators tried to "play tricks" on Hart to get him mad and hopefully thrown out of the race. Englehardt caught a man trying to fling pepper in Hart's eyes and the angry race director stepped in and decked the man to the ground. He then told everyone to leave Hart alone or else they would receive the same punishment.

Hart held onto the lead for hours. "Hichborn (Hart), is in fine order, being trained down to good condition, with clean limbs, without an ounce of superfluous flesh. He showed good speed and wind." After 20 hours, he reached 90 miles and had a commanding lead. "The sight was novel and interesting as the varied-colored animated humanity went round

Boston Music Hall

and round the hall." To the great surprise of the spectators, Hart won the race with 119 miles in 30 hours, winning the Englehardt Medal and the $100.

The Bean Pot Tramp

Hart proved that his victory wasn't a fluke when three weeks later, on May 14, 1879, he won a 50-mile race at Lowell, Massachusetts in 8:50.

He had earned a spot in the Interstate Beanpot competition, representing Massachusetts. This was a relay tournament between teams from Massachusetts, Maine, and Rhode Island, called, "The Bean Pot Tramp" held in a mammoth tent at the Riding Academy in Back Bay, Boston. Each state's team consisted of twelve runners. Every day, for six

Back Bay from the State House 1857

days, two runners on each team ran for six hours each. Maine came out on top, but Hart ran the second furthest of all the runners, more than 39 miles, earning him the respect of the sport in New England.

THE BEAN POT.

The Colored Pedestrian Distances all his Competitors.

For the final week of the tournament, Hart competed in a six-day walking match with twenty others. He put on an impressive performance. On day four, running in third place, he competed in an ad hoc sprint against **Joseph E. Coughlin** (1853-) of Warwick, Massachusetts. Coughlin tripped and fell on the track and made the accusation that Hart had intentionally tripped him. Hart insisted it was accidental. He was almost disqualified until Coughlin withdrew his protest.

The last day turned into a fierce race between **Richard Lacouse** (1848-1923), and Hart. Both had spells where they collapsed on the track

The following is a list of the successful contestants and the prizes:

1st Prize—Lacouse, 427 miles.......................... $300
2d Prize—Hichborn, 424 miles, 5 laps.............. 150
3d Prize—Coughlin, 400 miles........................ 100
4th Prize—Wheeler, 356 miles......................... 75
5th Prize—Durgin, 338 miles........................... 50
6th Prize—O'Connor, 329 miles, 3 laps............ 25
7th Prize—Hurley, 319 miles........................... 15

due to the intense heat inside the tent. Hart's episode was serious. "Every effort was made to revive him, as he was only a few laps behind Lacouse, although it was thought for a time that he was dead, and after about an hour and a half of unceasing efforts, he revived sufficiently to warrant a removal to his house." Lacouse ran only a few more laps when he also collapsed, but he held on for the win of 427 miles, to Hart's 424. Hart won $150 and came away with a sprained knee.

Daniel O'Leary Starts Training Hart

On July 23-26, 1879, Hart placed an impressive second place at O'Leary's six-day, 75-hour race held in Boston's Music Hall, promoted by Engelhardt. That success got the attention of famous American pedestrian, **Daniel O'Leary** (1846-1933) of Chicago, who took Hart under his wing to train and back financially. O'Leary had faced discrimination as an Irish American. He had become a

Hart and O'Leary

leading advocate of women in the sport and now became a supporter of Hart, helping him overcome racial prejudice against him. O'Leary spent a couple of months with Hart, "giving him information about walking and advancing his interests." Soon Hart would be given the nickname "Black Dan" or "Young Dan" which was a huge compliment during that era -- a black and younger version of the best early pedestrian, Daniel O'Leary.

Plans were coming together for the 5th Astley Belt six-day race to be held in Madison Square Garden. The Astley Belt races were a series of world championship six-day races that had been established by Englishman **Sir John Dugdale Astley** (1828-1894) in early 1878.

Originally the 5th race in the series was supposed to be held in October 1879, but the British moved it up to September. **Edward Payson Weston** was the current holder of the Astley Belt and the six-day world record holder with 550 miles. O'Leary entered Hart in the race which was an "astonishment" to the manager of the race, **Charles D. Hess** (1838-1909), who thought the entry of the black runner "seemed strange" and should have been approved by the Astley managers in London. This was a major

Edward Payson Weston

development, for a black runner to compete for the greatest prize in the sport, on the biggest stage at Madison Square Garden. There had been other black pedestrians in the sport before Hart, but none had yet competed at this level. On August 5, 1879, a cable with £100 was sent to *Sporting Life* in London to secure Hart's entry.

The news went around the country that a "Boston negro" was going to compete. O'Leary seriously coached him to get ready for the race. Public relations were also important to get Hart in front of the public. He put on an eight-mile exhibition run as a warmup act before a featured 75-hour race at Allston Hall in Boston.

Providence, Rhode Island Race

Unwisely, two weeks before the Astley Belt race, on Sep 8-13, 1879, Hart competed in a six-day 12.5 hours per day race at Providence, Rhode Island in Park Garden put on by O'Leary. When he had originally entered this race, it was thought that the Astley Belt race would be held weeks later but then it was moved up. Hart won the Providence race easily with 362 miles, pleasing his friends, and proving that he was worthy to compete for the Astley Belt. It was pointed out that he beat eleven "white competitors." He won $300, a gold chain, and a solid silver belt and then rested until the next race.

Pedestrians Protest Against Hart

Five days before the Fifth Astley Belt Race, a pre-race meeting was held in New York City, at the office of *Turf, Field, and Farm*, attended by Hart. The first  agenda item was whether Hart, a "colored ped" should be allowed to run. "Objections were made on account of Hart's color, and a letter of protest from **Edward Payson Weston** had been presented. Weston argued that the white competitors ought not to be compelled to associate with a negro on the track."

George W. Atkinson, of the *Sporting Life* in London, overseeing the race for John Astley said, "without hesitation" that Hart would not be excluded, and quoted race rules that stated any man could enter who deposited £100. One of the men present said, "Do you call that (n-word) a man?" Englehardt, Hart's backer, spoke up and said, "You will find that Frank Hart is a pretty good man." That cut off the racist discussion. Hart signed the race agreement and was given a round of applause. He stated that he had recovered from his six-day race the prior week and hoped it would not hurt his chances. Englehart said, "I hardly expect he will come in first, though there is no telling beforehand. I do expect, however, that he will get a good place."

Fifth Astley Belt Race

The races for the Astley Belt were the most prestigious six-day races of the era. Daniel O'Leary of Chicago won the first two Astley Belt Races. **Charles Rowell** (1852-1902) of England, won the Third Astley Belt Race and brought the belt back to England. Edward Payson Weston won the fourth race and would defend the belt on September 22, 1879, in Madison Square Garden, New York City.

More than 250 men went to work preparing Madison Square Garden for the race. They constructed the track, built the stands, and put down new flooring. "The pedestrians will be accommodated in tents placed around the inside of the track. The stand for the scorers, judges, and reporters was built in three tiers."

An Astley Belt pre-race description was published that included: "Frank Hart, the colored boy is a full-blooded Haitian negro. He is a round-faced, copper-colored, boyish-looking fellow, and looks uncomfortable in the good clothes that have been bought for him. He is 22 years of age, reads and writes, weighs about 140 pounds, and is credited with a great deal of shrewdness, pluck, and modesty."

The Fifth Astley Belt race began with thirteen starters on September 22, 1879, in front of several thousand people. When the contestants appeared, O'Leary was at Hart's side, giving him support. Hart was dressed in a gray shirt and black pants. All contestants

wore large numbers painted in red on black oilskin bibs on their chests. Shortly after midnight, the word "go" was given and off they went, with **George Hazael** (1845-1911), of England, running fast in the lead.

Hart Dogs Rowell

Early on, at the instructions of O'Leary, Hart dogged the heels of former champion Rowell of England, staying just a few feet behind him around the track. Rowell, who had used this strategy in the past against others, did not like it done to him. He tried to shake Hart off by sprinting at times, but Hart stuck with him in second place. This made Hart a quick favorite among the New York crowd who wanted to see the Englishman lose and cheered Hart repeatedly. A man said, "Turning the tables is fair play. That's the game Rowell played on O'Leary on this very track when he first won the belt." Another man replied, "Rowell wouldn't care a button if they had the entire colored race behind him in a string. He's come here to win that belt and all the money that goes with it."

Hart's backers had thought he would receive racist taunts. "He had been cautioned by his backers to pay no heed to insults, and not let them disturb his equanimity, but to his surprise, the spectators treated him with almost unvarying courtesy, and he encountered no taunts." A drunken man did start to yell that "the colored man" should be taken off the track. The police quickly ejected the man from the building. The black spectators in the audience gathered and showed their

appreciation by cheering for all the runners, not just Hart.

The news press was curious about Hart. "The colored boy Hart chews on a quill, and plods along at a rattling pace." They were surprised that he increasingly became a great favorite, was repeatedly cheered by the crowd and received more bouquets of flowers than any other runner. Hart, who did not grow up in the South, thought it was funny that the newspapers called him a "boy" since he was 22 years old with a family.

After sixty miles, Hart gave up on trying to annoy Rowell and stuck to his own pace, fighting off cramps. "The colored youth has created more surprise than any of the other walkers. O'Leary has taken a great interest in the boy, and Hart has imitated the late champion to such perfection. He even carries the corn cobs, after the manner of his preceptor. He walks and runs most gracefully." Some bystanders called him "a smoked Irishman." **Judge John Callahan**, of the district court of New York, said that Hart was no negro at all, but O'Leary painted. Hart ignored it all, never complained, and implicitly obeyed O'Leary's advice, who at

times would dart out, run along with Hart, encouraging him on.

Hart received many big bouquets of flowers from spectators, including two magnificent floral horseshoes, which were put above the entrance to his tent. One had the words in flowers, "Go it, Black Dan!" Inside were two small tables covered with "Florida water, perfumed soap, a toothbrush, a hairbrush and comb, a bag of pears, some grapes, oatmeal, ginger snaps, calves' foot jelly, crackers, eggs, a bottle of milk, a kerosene stove, and an earthen teapot. Hart's clothes hung upon a line stretched across the tent. Everything was as neat as a bandbox."

Many black spectators came out to cheer him on. Hundreds of people stood outside the building trying to get glimpses

FOLLOWS:

THE SCORE AT MIDNIGHT.

Rowell	127	Hazael	100
Guyon	115	Jackson	78
Ennis	102	Weston	92
Hart	107	Taylor	80
Merritt	104	Krohne	90
Panchot	100	Federmeyer	81

of the runners on the track through the open doors. Sportsmen doubted that he would last beyond three days, especially because of his recent six-day race in Rhode Island. He reached 100 miles in about 21 hours, 110 miles in 24 hours, and was in third place. Rowell covered 127 miles during the first 24 hours.

On day two, after his 126th mile, Hart fell on the track and a crowd rushed to see him. O'Leary was quickly at his side, and he was carried to a nearby tent. He complained of giddiness and pains in his stomach. A rumor circulated that he had been drugged by outsiders, but O'Leary didn't believe it. An hour later Hart recovered and returned to the track. Betters were starting to place wagers on Hart.

Hart later looked fresh and lively and attracted the applause of the whole building again and again. Hart was asked how he felt about the new nickname that was given to him, "Black Dan." He said, "I hope Mr. O'Leary won't be offended by it.

	Miles.
Rowell	215
Guyon	200
Merritt	197
Hart	193
Hazael	186
Ennis	180
Weston	173
Krohne	160
Jackson	160
Panchot	154
Ferdermeyer	150
Taylor	100

I am very proud of it." When asked how he was being treated, he replied, "Splendid. The people are very friendly to me, very nice. See how they applaud any little thing. Wait until I win and then they may cheer me all they like, and I'll like it too. When I'm on the track and see all the faces and hear the music and the scores, I feel every step I take is bringing me so much nearer. I have a burning desire to get that belt." After 48 hours, Hart was in fourth place with 193 miles. Rowell had 215 miles.

Early in the morning of the third day, Hart was rolled up in blankets, put into a cab, and taken to a Turkish bath. "He slept while they were undressing him, during the bath, all through the shampooing, in the hot room, until they brought him out to cool on the canvas, and only woke up when they turned the cold water on his face. He then started with a jump and made a rush as though to get on the track and resume his march."

Back at the track, he ate a breakfast of two mutton chops, a little bit of beefsteak, a large plate of chopped-up eggs, six pieces of toast, cornbread, and tea. He was worried about eating so much, and not leaving anything for the others. "To see him in his tent eating was as amusing a sight as can be imagined.

	Miles.
Rowell	310
Merritt	281
Hazael	276
Hart	273
Guyon	270
Weston	251
Krohne	233
Jackson	230
Ennis	220
Ferdemeyer	220
Panchot	205
Taylor	150

He often laughed at the idea of being waited on by white men."

Fred Englehardt, who was on this team, assured him that it was a pleasure to help such a good-natured chap. "While Hart sat at the little table, his eyes sparkling with delight, he knocked his knuckles on the table and with much formality called out, 'Waiter, some water.' When the meal was finished, he took his favorite toothpick from behind his ear, and as he lounged back in his chair, he looked sternly and said, 'Give me my bill, and hurry up.' Then breaking out into a ripple of laughter, he jumped up, shook himself, and with 'This is bully,' dashed out on the track again. A merrier, harder working little chap than Hart cannot be imagined."

Hart was told that Weston thought he was the best man on the track, which was a surprise because he initially didn't want Hart in the competition because he was black. Hart felt honored by that compliment. He returned to the track to cheers of, "Go it, Dan! Fetch 'em up! Give it to 'em!" His eyes would brighten when the band played, "Baby Mine." At the end of day three, Hart was still in fourth place, with 273 miles. Rowell was leading with 310.

On the fourth day, it bugged Hart to see Hazael running past him, increasing his lead. He became impatient, wanting to run after him, but both O'Leary and Englehardt insisted that he continued walking. In the early morning, they finally let him go ahead and run. Hart and Hazael started racing around the track. Sadly, while rounding a turn, Hart twisted his right ankle and fell to the ground very awkwardly. O'Leary was quickly on the track. Hart thought it was just a stumble and wanted to continue, but he was carried to his tent where his already swelling ankle was treated for two hours before he resumed his walk.

Hart still struggled and, "crawled around the track at a snail's pace. His lips were bloodless, his eyes dim, and his limbs trembled beneath him at every step." His trainer called him back into his tent for some needed rest.

The thousands of spectators in the Garden were being well-fed. "Sandwiches 3,000 per day; pork and beans 300 pounds of pork and two bushels of beans a day; hams, 50 a day; corned beef, 200 pounds a day; pigs' feet 4,000 sold up to noon; pickled tongues, 6,300; pies, 250 every 24 hours; java coffee, 200 pounds; oysters, 5,000 a day; roast beef, 100 pounds a day. In addition to these, there have been many thousands of barrels of chicken and lobster salad consumed, along with several thousand kegs of beer."

	No. of Miles.
Rowell	402
Hazael	368
Merritt	367
Guyon	345
Hart	339
Weston	322
Ennis	310
Krohne	307
Ferdemeyer	288
Taylor	180

Rowell reached 402 miles by the end of day four, and Hart reached 339 miles and had fallen to fifth place. Outside of the building, racist comments were heard against Hart that were not appreciated by black friends who had money on their new hero.

During the long early morning hours of day five, a cry was heard from Hart's tent, "Put him out!" People feared that someone was trying to assault Hart. But soon Englehardt appeared at the door of the canvas house and assured everyone that Hart was fine. "He explained that one of the attendants who had not slept for several nights, who was in the act of cooking Hart's supper, had

laid his head on his hand for a moment on the table beside the gas stove and his hat took fire. One side of his head was in flames, but he slept on and took no notice of it." They rescued the man and "put him out." Such were the hazards of being on a 19th-century crew.

The attention of Hart's crew was impressive. "When the colored boy drew back the flap of the tent and entered, the men in there were lounging in chairs or lying on the floor. The moment they saw him, they were on their feet. Two of them took him in their arms and laid him on the cot bed as gently, as kindly, as tenderly and with as much care as if he were the son of a duchess, or better still, their own flesh and blood. It was an exquisite scene, and it brought out qualities that did honor to human nature."

A well-known trainer was asked who he thought was the best walker on the track. His reply was, "Black Dan, without any doubt. That boy has not had a fair show here. He ran a race only a week before he came in here. It's amazing to see what he is doing. It's my opinion, Dan will wear the belt yet."

WAS ROWELL POISONED ?

His Sudden Illness and What He Says About It.

A DAY OF EXCITEMENT.

The event of the day that received the most attention was when the race leader, Rowell became seriously sick and believed that he had been poisoned by someone trying to make him fail. He had eaten some grapes that had been handed over the rail to him by a spectator and then began to feel hot and sick with sore eyes. After five hours of being treated by his trainers and a doctor, Rowell returned to the track, still holding the lead, and looked somewhat pale. Hart felt great sympathy for him, expressed his sorrow, and gave him a picture of himself as a gift. Rowell said, "Thank you, old fellow." Rowell felt he could still win but was disappointed that the 600-mile barrier looked like it was now out of his reach.

Hart also was given grapes and a tempting-looking banana, perhaps by the same man. He had wanted to eat the banana but remembered O'Leary's firm instructions about being careful where he obtained food, handed the food over to his trainer, and it was thrown away. Other runners received the suspect grapes but also did not eat them.

During the evening, Hart dogged the heels of Edward Payson Weston who was about ten miles behind him. A typical racist treatment of the time could be read in the *New York Daily Herald*. "Why look at the darkey! See him sidle up beside

	Miles.
Rowell	453
Merritt	442
Hazael	436
Hart	415
Guyon	415
Weston	405
Krohne	382
Ennis	378
Ferdemeyer	348
Taylor	213

Weston. Up they come, walking like shot, the darkey just a step behind the actor and watching him like a thief." Weston was very annoyed with Hart's dogging and turned around

showing a "puffed face" at Hart and complained to O'Leary. For ten minutes this went on until Weston finally left the track for his tent and Hart followed, almost also going into the tent, causing the crowd to roar with laughter. At the end of day five, Hart was in fourth place with 415 miles. Rowell had 453 miles with an eleven-mile lead on the rest of the field

On the final day, Hart fought hard to keep fourth place, running ahead of **George W. Guyon** (1853-1933) of Chicago, Illinois. It was a continuous fight between the two. "First, one would force the pace to run and then the other. This was just what people enjoyed, and

they did what they could to urge them on." Eventually, Hart got an advantage while Guyon was in his tent and the lead increased to three miles.

O'Leary was pleased with Hart's performance and said, "If he had not sprained his ankle, he would have done much better, but as it is he is making a good race. He is receiving telegrams and letters from all over the country and flowers and presents are pouring in by the bushel. Hart is a good boy, and I am fond of him. He will make his fortune at walking."

The building was filled with thousands of people. "A ceaseless human tide streamed in every minute through the great main entrance. Every seat was taken up. You can scarcely get within six feet of either rail. All the narrower walks were blocked and impassable. The great central arena was alive with one moving, shouting mass."

Twelve Thousand People Watching the Last Laps.

When Hart ran past 450 miles, the crowd shouted with great enthusiasm. By achieving that milestone, he would have a share of the gate receipts. Guyon was also trying to reach 450 miles and was very annoyed when Hart seemed to block his efforts to pass him. He even complained to the referee, **George W. Atkinson**, who gave him a warning. O'Leary encouraged him on to dog Guyon's heels. O'Leary ran behind Hart, clapping his hands, telling him to run faster. Finally, Guyon had enough of being pestered and retired to his tent. One reporter, hoping for Hart's failure wrote, "The whole thing was looked on as a mean trick of the colored boy to secure an unfair advantage, as Guyon is by far the better of the two."

Oleary was disgusted with how many of the runners were dressed. He later said, "The bathing drawers and circus trunks worn by the majority of the men on the track are not fit for pedestrian's dress. There should be a small pair of regular pantaloons coming part of the way down the thigh." Weston's strange antics to get attention were also thought to give the sport a bad name. "Weston was ambling around the track, playing queer antics, and twisting his body into all sorts of apish forms, to the great amusement of a few and to the great disgust of the many. He was hissed and cheered alternately as he passed around the track, and in some instances, insulting epithets were hurled at him by ruffians in the crowd."

THE AGONY OVER.

And Charley Rowell Takes Away the Astley Belt.

In the end, the Englishman, Rowell won the Astley Belt again with 530 miles. "A perfect roar went up from all sides as Rowell passed along with the Stars and Stripes over his shoulders. Cheer after cheer went up until all else was drowned. People grew frantic with excitement and stood upon one another in an eager effort to see the track. Hats were thrown in the air, handkerchiefs waved, and feet stamped, until the very building shook. The dust and smoke

	Miles.	Best Pre- vious Score.
Rowell	530	500
Merritt	515	475
Hazael	500	492
Hart	482	424
Guyon	470	480
Weston	455	550
Ennis	450	475
Krohne	450	461
Taylor	250	(No record.)

rushed upward in volumes so dense that even the electric lights paled and seemed to flicker."

Hart had held onto fourth place, finishing with 482 miles, twelve miles ahead of Guyon, and 27 miles ahead of legendary Weston. The band played, "Home Sweet Home," and the audience started to leave the building. "It was no small matter to get an audience of something like 10,000 persons out of five narrow doors, and it was more than half an hour before everybody was out. The crush at the doors was tremendous, and thousands strolled about the house waiting wisely for a turn. Small boys and ambitious young men walked short spurts on the track and looked curiously at the tents, but at length, everybody was out, as well as the lights."

FRANK HART—

Hart smiled and walked into his tent with the air of a champion. He sat down on a chair, stretched his legs out before him, closed his eyes, and sank back on the chair. Someone pulled a joke and yelled "tickets" causing Hart to rouse startled. O'Leary said, "Well, Frank, you've done well." Hart smiled and replied, "The only thing I am sorry for is that the belt is going back to England."

While Hart's team was preparing to leave the building, he chatted pleasantly with those surrounding him. He said he was not tired and felt first-rate. He did admit that he was a little sleepy but thought he could have continued to walk many more miles if needed. Looking at the mass of floral arrangements around his tent, he guessed that he would have to hire an express wagon to get them all home. When it was time to go, Hart walked out of the 27th Street entrance of Madison Square Garden between his trainers where a carriage was waiting for him. "The crowd cheered him as he passed, and hundreds of pleasant words that were sent after him seemed to please him. He got into the carriage with O'Leary and Engelhardt, and as soon as the door was closed sank back on the cushions and closing his eyes, said, 'My, wasn't that a crowd. Never saw such a big crowd in all my life!'"

As the carriage drove down the road, a crowd of adoring fans followed and tried their best to see him through the window. When he reached St. Omer Hotel, a policeman had to clear the sidewalk so he could enter the hotel. On reaching his room, he was asked what he wanted. He requested stewed kidneys, buttered toast, tea, and some mincemeat pie. His massive amount of flower bouquets filled a parlor in the hotel.

St. Omer Hotel

Hart Returned to Boston as a Hero

The next day, Hart arrived by train back in Boston and was met by a large crowd at the depot which pleased him. Asked how he felt, he replied, "I am all right, feel good, and should feel so, as I am satisfied that my fellow citizens have appreciated my efforts to recapture the belt." A banquet was held that evening in his honor, "participated in not only by citizens of his own color but by all true Americans"

Frank Hart, the first truly successful black ultrarunner, had competed on the world's biggest stage. The world was surprised and noticed. "Hart, the negro, who entered the contest almost under protest, and who was looked upon almost slightingly by his fellows on the track, won not only a good record and place but that which was of greater value, respect, and admiration for his modest, manly bearing and plucky work. To be less than fifty miles behind the winner under the circumstances is a magnificent record, and the ablest pedestrians may well regard with apprehension this healthy, lively fellow, who is so heartily in love with his work, and who instead of saving himself, seems always to have vitality to spare."

After his exhausting, surprising, six-day Astley Belt performance, Hart wisely took time off from competing in races but put on exhibitions at races for a couple of months. "Frank Hart of the late Astley belt contest came on the track and gave some very pretty exhibition spins. He was loudly cheered, not alone by the audience, but also by the pedestrians on the track." Receptions were held in his honor, including one put on by the Centennial Club of Cambridge, Massachusetts held at Payne Memorial Hall. He was given an elegant solid silver water service by his Boston friends.

PAYNE MEMORIAL BUILDING.

Outside of Boston, Hart had his critics. In Chicago, it was falsely reported that during the recent Astley Belt race, he had been forced to run like a slave. "His trainers forced the negro pedestrian to keep upon the track. He was wretchedly exhausted and made repeated efforts to escape from the ring, but as often they compelled him to go on with the idiotic self-torment." In New York, they praised him but considered him to be an exception to his race. "This dusky young Apollo is a picture of grace and power. It is not the physique that we associate with men of his color. There is none of the slouch of the plantation about him. He is in earnest, with just intent on his work."

O'Leary said, "Frank is a good boy, and I have no reason to regret taking the interest in him I have. We had no trouble with him to speak of." Spectators paid more than $70,000 for tickets during the week. For his effort, Hart won a staggering $3,750 valued at $111,000 today. Controversy arose when the track was remeasured and discovered to be short, crediting runners five miles or more extra distance. Hart wanted the results corrected, which would have caused three runners to come up short of miles needed to earn a share of the gate money, giving Hart about $390 more. He hired a lawyer and sued the race promoters. Anyway, Hart was now a very rich man, and this was only the beginning of his fame and fortunes yet to come.

In Washington D.C., thoughts were political. "It is now intimated that Hart, the colored walkist should have been nominated for Governor in Massachusetts. He shows remarkable running powers."

People were stunned at how much money Hart won. "Won't some philanthropic stalwart at once organize a bank to take care of his money for him? A kind of a Freedman's Bank."

Frank Hart's Early Races

Date	City	Place	Miles	Place	Notes
Apr 25-26, 1879	Boston, MA	Music Hall	119	1	30 hour. $100
May 14, 1879	Lowell, MA	Huntington Hall	50	1	50-miler 8:50
May 21, 1879	Boston, MA	Mammoth Tent	39	2	Beanpot, $45
May 26-31, 1879	Boston, MA	Mammoth Tent	424	1	six-day, Interstate, $150
Jul 23-26, 1879	Boston, MA	Music Hall	263	2	75-hour 3 day, $150
Sep 8-13, 1879	Providence, RI	Park Garden	363	1	six-day, Champion Belt, $300
Sep 22-28, 1879	New York City, NY	Madison Square Garden	450	4	six-day, 5th Astley Belt, $3,750

CHAPTER TWO

World Record Holder

After the good training he received from O'Leary, and with his recent success, fame, and fortune, he was ready to go out on his own. He hired his own trainer/handler, **John D. Oliver** (1860-1914), age 19, who became better known as "Happy Jack Smith." Smith was originally from Richmond, Virginia, born to Irish parents. Within months he became recognized as the best pedestrian trainer in America. He developed a reputation for being able to keep his runners in the competition to the bitter end.

Hart also needed a manager/agent. He again turned to a very young, unproven, but dynamic talent. He hired nineteen-year-old **Jacob Julius "J.J." Gottlob** (1860-1933). Gottlob, a commercial traveler and theater man with west coast ties, took interest in pedestrianism. He would become known as the "Dean of Pacific Coast Theater managers." As he acquired money, he would be Hart's backer for several years.

The Rose Belt

With these two young men to look after him, in December 1879, Hart went to compete at the next big six-day tournament, the "Great International Six-Day Race" or "Rose Belt" held in Madison Square Garden in New York City. The manager of the  race was **Daniel Eugene Rose** (1846-1927) of New York City, a pedestrian promoter and owner of the D. E. Rose cigarette manufacturing company. This was perhaps the largest six-day race in history with 65 starters.

An expensive Rose Belt, valued at $400, was created for the winner, with seven rectangular sections. The center section included a globe with running figures and colored flags, and the words, "American International Champion of the World."

About 200 scorers were employed. Scores were displayed on dials for each runner. Each runner had a big number both on their chest and on their back. Hart was not the only black runner in the field, there were three others, **Edward Williams** of New York City, **Paul Molyneaux Hewlett** (1856-1891) of Boston, and **William H. Jacob Pegram** (1846-1913) of Boston, who would often run together with Hart on laps. Pegram was

Names.	Miles and Laps.	Names	Miles and Laps.
Panchot, P. J.	120	Roe, J.	86 7
Hart	117 2	Matthews	87 1
Hughes, John.	112	Brozie, S.	90
Faber, C.	112	McCormick, J.	90
Mahoney, J.	105	Williams, E.	89 8
Fitzpatrick, D.	105	Croft, Arthur.	89 3
Fitzgerald, P.	103 3	Webster, I.	84 4
Davis, Richard	103 1	Weaver, W. E.	87
Brody, Thos.	102	Ryan, W.	86 7
Russell S. P.	101	Murphy, Charles.	86 5
O'Brien, P.	101	Parris, A.	83 2
Panccot, H.	101	Lowery, John	85
Dufrane, George	100 2	Panchot, A.	83 7
Weaver, D.	100 1	Shannon, E.	82 7
Gideon, I.	100	Howard, Henry.	84 4
Krabne, P.	100	Gehring.	84
Geisert, E.	100	Murphy, James.	85
Illiton, G. T	100	Hadwater, George.	80
Campana, N.	100	Molyneaux, P.	80
Mignault, P.	100	Berdan, Chas.	79
Vint, Robert	100	McKee, D.	76 5
Hennessy, D. A.	94 3	Tompkins, A.	76 1
Walker, C.	94 7	Crawford, M.	69 2
Pegram, W.	95 7	Sprague, W.	69
Madden	95	Johnson, F.	64
Cow	95 1	Byrnes.	59
Reed	95	Gorman, T. W.	55 3
McClellan, J.	94 2	Davis, W. H.	53 3
LaCouse, H.	94	Brandes, Frederick	31 7
Madden	93 1	Cromwell, E.	44 5

a former slave from Sussex, Virginia. He won a small 60-hour race in Brighton, Massachusetts against whites, a month before Hart started competing. Pegram spoke in a thick southern black dialect that at times was mocked by the press.

After the first day, December 22, 1879, Hart was in second place with 117 miles. On day two, after **Peter J. Panchot** (1841-1917), of Buffalo, New York, withdrew from the race, Hart took over first place. By evening, only 48 of the 65 starters remained in the race.

Christian Faber

On Christmas Eve, day three, the race continued, and Hart lost the lead in the evening to **Christian Faber** (1848-1908), of Newark, New Jersey, when he went to get some sleep. Grumbles were heard by those with wagers on Hart, worried that he would not return. But Hart had not had very much sleep and needed it badly. He returned at midnight to kick off day four. Ten more runners chose to quit and celebrate their Christmas away from the Garden.

The largest crowd came out on Christmas Day (day four), with 7,000 people. "Hart looked the most wearied, and all his friends began to lose hope." He was in third place, but only two miles behind the leader. At 9 p.m., Hart, in his familiar striped suit, finally retook first place which caused the crowd to cheer. Hart's new trainer, **Happy Jack Smith** was pleased with his runner and said he was in "tip-top condition, determined to do or die." His goal was to exceed the 530 miles that **Charles Rowell** reached during the 5th Astley Belt a few months earlier. But his friends hoped that he would reach 551 miles, which would break **Edward Payson Weston's** world record of 550 miles.

Only 19 runners remained in the race. "The crowd at midnight had dwindled to a few hundred, and a good proportion of these were

stretched out on the upper benches for an all-night's sleep." Hart maintained a lead of six miles on day five which was close enough to push him hard.

ROWELL'S SCORE BEATEN

Hart, the Colored Boy, Wins with 540 Miles to his Credit.

On the last day, running through air foul with tobacco smoke, Hart became very excited when he reached his goal of 531 miles. "Hart was swinging around with an American flag amid tremendous cheering, that was aroused by a dog trot into which he struck with the ease and lightness of a fresh man on the track."

Hart, fueling on champagne diluted in seltzer, cruised to victory wearing a white flannel suit, with a blue jockey cap on

his head. He reached 540.1 miles, running the last lap with the Rose Belt around his waist, carrying an American flag. Cheers rang out that shook the building. His mark was the third-best six-day mark in the world at that point and the best accomplished on American soil. Eight runners had exceeded 500 miles in the race. Three of the black runners finished in the top seven. Hart had established himself as a world elite ultrarunner and went away with at least $3,000 of winnings and the Rose Belt valued at $400.

It was challenging for large crowds to exit Madison Square Garden because of its few narrow doors. "There was a tremendous crush at all the doors when the crowd was leaving the Garden. At the Madison Avenue exit, two women fainted. They were carried into the street by their escorts, and were taken to a neighboring drug store, where restoratives were applied."

Sadly, one of the contestants, **Clarence G. Howard** (1859-1879) who had withdrawn from the race on day one after 75 miles, feeling sick, died four days later at his home on Long Island. "Everything possible was done to save him, but without avail, and he died from utter exhaustion. He was more like a schoolteacher or a man of sedentary employment than a professional walker."

Reaction and Racism

The New York Daily Herald wrote, "The promise of the young negro Hart to become one of the leading pedestrians of the world was handsomely fulfilled on Saturday night when the boy retired from the track with 540 miles to his credit." The reporter speculated in the racist attitude of the day, that Hart was successful because he was "docile and obedient" to his trainers late into the race and gained his perfect walking method from his "master," O'Leary. But the article then admitted, "As for Hart himself, his manners and achievements have made him as popular as any pedestrian in America and he may confidently challenge any other pedestrian in the world."

When seen the next day, Hart said, "I felt rather stiff in my joints when Jack Smith, my trainer, pulled me from my bed and had a sort of headache, which I suppose is due to the wine I drank last evening to keep me awake. A spin of a mile or so though put me all right."

FRANK HART

Received by the Sporting Fraternity of Boston.

Is Made the Victim of a Banquet and Speeches.

Hart returned to Boston by train and was greeted by a large crowd at the Old Colony depot. A few days later, a nice banquet was held in his honor with many dignitaries giving flattering speeches.

Much of the nation was astonished that a black man could rise to be the greatest American athlete in the most popular spectator sport of that era. *The Boston Globe* wrote, "We have heard it said that the negro was incapable of noble endeavor. Hart has proven the lie to this assertion, for he has not only vanquished 49 white men but beaten the remaining sixteen who pluckily continued on the track. Great deeds accomplished by one man tend to raise the race to which that man belongs in public estimation. Hart's success must be a natural spur of grand and nobler achievements. His great zeal, devotion, and honesty of purpose displayed on every occasion, he has earned for himself the exalted position of champion of America, if not of the world."

Hart, the Colored Boy, Wins with 540 Miles to his Credit.

In addressing the racism of the day, *The Brooklyn Daily Eagle* wrote, "Mr. Hart has shown conclusively that there is nothing in a black skin or wooly hair that is incompatible with fortitude. The idea that our colored brother is an inferior will never sustain so severe a shock at the hands of the logician as it will when a colored man proves his physical equality as Hart has done. In the contest which ended last night, there were Americans, Englishmen, Irishmen, and Germans and this colored boy showed that he was above their average."

Hart was now very rich, with winnings of at least $5,000, valued at $145,000 today. He believed that his financial backers had cheated him of some of his past earnings. One reporter warned, "He is in danger of falling into bad hands, owing to a disposition to be guided by other people instead of relying upon his own knowledge." He became determined to take ownership and be his own backer. In January 1880, he looked at proposals to compete in San Francisco and then in Australia. He participated in some exhibition runs and announced intentions to run in the 2nd O'Leary Belt to be held in April 1880 in Madison Square Garden.

On Feb 26, 1880, a son was born to the Harts in their home at 26 North Anderson Street in Boston. They named him **William Walter Hart**. Hart gave his occupation on the birth record as "Pedestrian."

The Second O'Leary Belt

Daniel O'Leary established the "Oleary Belt" six-day race series in October 1879 as an American championship alternative to the Astley Belt Race. The British had too much control over the Astley Belt series and this American version could prepare American runners to compete on a world stage without traveling to England. The O'Leary belt race series could only be competed in America. The first O'Leary Belt was won by eighteen-year-old, **Nicholas Murphy** (1861-1904) of Haverstraw, New York, who reached 505 miles. Six months later, it was time for the Second Astley Belt race.

THE O'LEARY BELT.

THE SIX-DAY PEDESTRIAN CHAMPIONSHIP OF AMERICA.

A SWEEPSTAKES OF $9,000 and, one-half the gate-money, with a special prize of $1,000 if the best record is beaten.

18 COMPETITORS HAVE ENTERED FOR THE CONTEST, (9 OF WHOM HAVE RECORDS OF 500 MILES AND OVER,) viz.:

Nicholas Murphy, present champion; P. McIntyre, champion of California; Frank H. Hart, John Ennis, F. Krohne, C. Faber, W. Pegram, S. Merritt, E. Williams, Harry Howard, Jos. Allen, J. Dobler, G. Hanwaker, J. Henry, Mr. Jaybee, J. F. Brown, W. H. Kerwin, and J. Woods.

This great event commences

MONDAY, April 5, 1880, at 12:05 A. M.,
at
MADISON-SQUARE GARDEN.

GRAND SACRED CONCERT, SUNDAY NIGHT,
April 4, commencing 9 P. M.

Admission..50 cents

At 11:30 p.m., on April 4, 1880, Hart, age 23, entered Madison Square Garden and walked around the track to his tent while given loud applause from 6,000 people. He was confident that he would win and was a 3-1 favorite among the betters, and had boasted to the press, "I'll break those white fellow's hearts, I will. You hear me!" At midnight, all the 18 starters lined up and pedestrian promoter and referee, **William B. Curtis** (1837-1900) shouted the word, "Go." The competitors went off on a trot or dead run, with **Edward Williams,** another black runner, finishing in the first mile in 6:20 with the lead. After an hour, the third black runner, **William Pegram**, was in the lead. He had been called, "the dark horse" of the race. By morning, nearly 8,000 spectators filled the Garden. At the rail, the beer-drinking, and cigarette-smoking men puffed their smoke into the faces of the plodding pedestrians as they passed by.

"Pegram and Williams, the dark team of Hart's nationality, moved steadily and untiringly in the procession, at times working up and making a tandem with Black Dan as leader." Some commented that Hart was coaching Pegram as they ran.

Hart reached 100 miles in 16:58:55 and covered an amazing 131 miles on the first day. He held first place by two miles over **John Dobler** (1859-) of Chicago, who had been training with O'Leary and had been dogging Hart's steps. "Hart's fine form, together with his stylish elastic walk and graceful carriage, won him much favor among the fair sex. He has since the last walk grown a mustache." He finished day two with 225 miles.

John Dobler

Some observers closely watched Hart to find possible flaws. But what they found was impressive. "Hart is of a bright and happy temperament. He was always ready to look at whatever was going on, to chat with a contestant and glance in the direction from which an encouraging shout came, to give a weary plodder a kind word and helping arm, and to laugh at the fun which was going on."

On day three, Hart feasted primarily on beef tea, mutton tea, and chicken tea. He also ordered quail on toast. "An hour later Hart was seen crunching a big

WONDERS OF THE BIG WALK.

HART AND DOBLER STILL GOING MORE THAN 100 MILES A DAY.

piece of pie, the crust of which shone with grease. Although traveling fast, he took a mouthful about every three steps, with seemly great relish. His food is kept outside of his tent in a refrigerator and either Happy Jack or one of his assistants keep an arm over it constantly." He reached 300 miles in an American record 66:28 and finished off the day with 315 miles, three miles behind Dobler.

Day four presented a furious battle between Hart and Dobler. "The sharpest struggle of the race took place. Dobler began to quicken, and Hart followed. Lap after lap was covered and still the young Chicagoan hurried the work, which evidently began to surprise Hart, who was immediately behind him." By mid-morning, the battle seriously exhausted Hart.

Later in the day, Dobler "hit the wall" and broke down, allowing Hart to build a double-digit lead in miles by late evening. The smoke in the Garden became terribly thick. When the walkers finally complained, the windows were opened.

It soon was discovered that smoke was coming up through cracks in the floor of the scorer's box. A smoldering fire was found below that had been lit by a watchman trying to warm himself. It was put out and they were lucky it didn't spread throughout the building. Hart finished day four with 405 miles, ahead of the world record pace, and a 14-mile lead.  The press was amazed to see the two black runners, Hart and Pegram leading the race. When Hart started to have fainting spells, his trainers gave him stimulants and a "magic sponge" to revive him.

On day five, Hart concentrated on keeping his lead over his friend Pegram. They raced hard against each other for about seven miles during the morning without a break. "Although Hart was literally 13 miles ahead in the journey, he dogged Pegram's footsteps relentlessly. Pegram lost his temper at times, occasionally throwing his broad feet backward like scoops and showering Hart's legs with sawdust. Hart took this good-naturedly, retaliating by giving Pegram a brisk brush once in a while." Runners could reverse direction for the next lap at the scorers' table whenever they wanted. Hart would at times reverse direction without Pegram immediately noticing, causing him confusion and to the delight of the laughing crowd. At the end of day five, Hart reached 492 miles, with a 19-mile lead over Pegram.

World Record

As Hart started the final day, he struggled. **Happy Jack Smith** said, "At first, Frank was terribly sick and tired. He didn't want to work. He was awful leg weary. But he said he had to get that belt, and he went on."

Hart reached 500 miles early in the morning, two miles ahead of the world-record pace. His tent was nearly hidden by all the flowers that had been presented to him. He reached 550 miles with about six hours to go. "This was the signal for a perfect storm of applause from the men and boys, while the women waved handkerchiefs and shook their fans in a perfect frenzy of excitement. As he neared his tent, in the next lap, the colored favorite grasped an American flag from the hands of one of his trainers and ran at a lively gait around the track for the next lap, waving the flag in the air, amid the yells and cheers of the crowd." The Garden was packed to capacity including many black spectators who had come to witness Hart's victory.

HART LEADS THE WORLD.

BEATING ENGLAND'S BEST RECORD WITH TWELVE MILES TO SPARE.

Three miles later Hart broke the world record of 553 miles, set by **Henry "Blower" Brown** (1843-1900) of England, two months earlier in London. This earned Hart a $1,000 bonus. "The yells and cheers which greeted him shook the building with their volume. Reaching his tent in the midst of the applause, he grasped a broom to which a flag was attached and ran the next lap as nimbly as a deer." Another described the sound as "it was more like a series of bloodthirsty war whoops than the cheering of a civilized multitude. Hart came bounding along like a yacht under full sail."

FRANK HART THE WINNER

AND ANOTHER BOSTON NEGRO SEC-OND IN THE RACE.

HART ROLLS UP 565 MILES BEFORE LEAVING THE TRACK, BEATING BROWN'S WORLD RECORD BY TWELVE MILES — PEGRAM THREE MILES AHEAD OF THE GREATEST AMERICAN RECORD — THE CLOSING HOURS OF THE GREAT WALK.

He didn't stop, wanting to pile up more miles. When he reached 560 miles, all eight runners still on the track joined him for a lap. Hart ran with a silk jockey cap of many colors that a spectator gave to him. For his final lap, he wore the O'Leary belt and waved the stars and stripes as the band played "Yankee Doodle." He finally retired after 141 hours and 23 minutes, with 565 miles, beating the previous world record by 12 miles.

O'Leary believed that Hart would break 600 miles someday. He said, "I am sure that he has not yet put his best foot forward. Look out for him in the next match." Pegram

	Mon.	Tue.	Wed.	Thr.	F.	Sat.	Total.
F. Hart	131	94	90	90	87	73	565
W. Pegram	104.6	94.2	100	91	83	70.7	543.7
H. Howard	97.4	97.4	88.7	94.1	78	81.5	534.5
J. Dobler	129	95	94	73	69	71	531
J. Allen	118.5	90.3	88	65	80	60.2	502.2
F. Krohne	82.2	94.6	89	85	88	78	516
E. Williams	100.1	74.7	80.2	93.5	87	73.5	509.5
G. Hazwater	90	76	75	73	69	68.3	450.3

reached 543 miles, for the third-best six-day score ever accomplished by an American up to that point, and the second-best performance on American soil.

Hart was driven by horse carriage to a Turkish bath, and after a nap of a couple of hours was taken to his agent's home nearby. "His trainer said that he had not a blister, chafe, or strain anywhere, and was good for another day's

BEST RECORDS IN SIX DAY MATCHES.
The following are the best records made in six day walks :

Name.		Miles.
Hart	New York, April, 1880,	565
Pegram	New York, April, 1880,	543
Brown	London, February, 1880,	553
Weston	London, June, 1879,	550
Rowell	New York, September, 1879,	524½
Hart	New York, December, 1879,	540 1-6
O'Leary	London, March, 1878,	520½
Murphy	New York, October, 1879,	505
Rowell	New York, March, 1879,	500
Hart	New York, September, 1879,	482

work at least as brisk as any he had done in the contest." Hart won an estimated $21,567 (including a wager on himself) valued at $627,000 today. His winnings so far during his running career exceeded $860,000 in today's value.

AFTER THE RACE.

How Frank Hart and the Great Pedestrians Felt the Day After Finishing the Great Walk.

The next day, when visited by a reporter, he was quietly smoking, sitting near a table displaying both his belts, the Rose Belt and the O'Leary Belt. "Hart looked the very picture of contentment with a quiet, easy dignity that well befits all heroes." He was surrounded by his agent, Gottlob, and his trainer, Happy Jack Smith. Daniel O'Leary arrived and they left together arm-in-arm to go celebrate at Putnam House with Pegram.

Reaction to Hart's World Record

There was a stunning racist reaction across the country that a black runner was the best ultrarunner in the world. In Louisiana: "Hart, the negro

HART WINS A SECOND BELT.

THE TWO NEGROES THE BEST TWO MEN.
END OF THE SIX-DAYS' WALK IN MADISON SQUARE
GARDEN—HART BEATS THE BEST RECORD, AND
SCORES FIVE HUNDRED AND SIXTY-FIVE MILES.

tramp, is the colored lion of the hour in New York. His legs have shown remarkable sustaining powers, and ladies give him bouquets." In Indiana, "The colored man's foot is not a thing to be despised. The negro walker carried off $16,000. Many a white man with a head full of brains never earned that much money in all his life."

In St. Louis, Missouri: "It is eminently proper that in a contest of this character that the honor should fall to a race celebrated for its physical accomplishments, as opposed to intellectual." In Kansas, "Legs pay better than brains every time. We, however, can't advise young men to cultivate a growth of legs rather than brains."

In England it was written, "The negro has now reappeared to public view in a new light. He has proved himself the 'champion long-distance pedestrian of the world.' This being an honour recently warmly contended for by many white men, it necessarily follows that to secure it must be a mark of unquestioned merit in the coloured men."

In Cleveland, Ohio: "It has always been claimed that the negro race was inferior to whites in every respect. But it appears that result of this match, that the negro race may lay claim to physical superiority to the white, in endurance of prolonged muscular exertion as in this walking match, and in the power of resisting tropical heat.

Frank Hart, a pioneer in competitive racewalking, poses with the O'Leary Belt in 1881.

The black race is evidently developing rapidly."

Tennessee described a reaction that was common in all the states: "Almost the sole topic of conversation among the colored people is the feat performed by the negro Frank Hart, and they seem quite proud of their champion."

Finally, a particularly cruel reaction printed in the *Agriculturalist* in Kansas directed at black migrants from the South, "If this knack of walking is by any means peculiar to colored people, we suggest that those of the Exodusters who are too lazy to work and have to be supported by charity, pick up their heels and walk back where they came from."

Migrants in Kansas referred to as Exodusters

Hart went with O'Leary on a victory tour to various cities, putting on walking exhibitions. O'Leary praised Hart's effect on others. "The colored boys are all crazy to walk, and darky pedestrians will probably soon be almost as numerous as blackberries in summer." O'Leary also expressed some racist observations that were common for the era, saying, "One great difficulty has been encountered in handling this class of men, and that is their desire for sleep. It gives the white man a decided advantage. The moment that night comes on, a terrible drowsiness is experienced that they cannot shake off without making a very great effort. With all his great score, Hart had to have his sleep, no matter how close the race might be."

Hart's prized belts went on display in a storefront in Boston. He turned his attention to putting together a contest against England's greatest champion, Charles Rowell. But the Brits were insistent that any such match be competed in England.

Serious Illness

Then tragedy struck. On about July 20, 1880, Hart became critically ill. Early on, a reporter visited him at his home at 26 North Anderson Street in Boston with a high fever. Hart said, "I feel much better today but my physician says I must keep quiet. Ice seems to be the only

Anderson Street, Boston

comfort that I have. My head worries me considerably, but I am satisfied that I will come out all right. It, however, annoys me, as I fear that it may hurt my chances for holding onto the O'Leary belt. But you can tell my friends that I hope to get out of my present sickness and show them that Boston's representative will not be behindhand at the next race."

FRANK HART,

The Champion Pedestrian, Reported to be Dangerously Ill.

After a few days, things got worse. "He spent a very restless night, and his family and friends are considerably exercised as the result. His trainer, **Happy Jack Smith**, arrived from New York and will watch him with his usual care. His presence seems to have given much confidence to the sick champion." His doctors diagnosed, "congestion of the brain," thought to have been caused by sunstroke. "Added to this, the great strain that he has endured by the loss of sleep in his tasks has been sufficient to affect his nervous system, which with excitement, has brought on the present fever." The press also speculated that he had typhoid fever.

Sarah	M. Hart	1	F	d	2	3	16	Tub. Meningitis 2 wks.	26 N. Anderson St.

Sarah Hart's Death Record

Adding to Hart's tragedy, his two-year-old daughter, Sarah, died on July 30, 1880, of "tuberculous meningitis" while Hart was still very low. She had been sick for two weeks. Hart likely had the same disease.

News of his illness spread across the country. Some editors were cruel. In Buffalo, New York, "Frank Hart, the peacock of pedestrians, the dandy of darkies, is sick with congestion of the brain. It is odd that the disease did not attack him in the legs." In Ottawa, Canada: "Frank Hart, the colored pedestrian, is dying in Boston. It is noticeable that men who force nature in any way, die young."

Smith tried to nurse Hart back to health, giving him alcoholic baths. After a few days, Smith reported Hart's condition. "I am glad to say Frank is much better tonight. He is more rational, but I do not yet consider him out of danger. I have followed the doctor's orders to the letter and allowed no one to see him. I will spare no expense to see Frank on his feet again. We'll take the starch out of those English blowers." Daniel O'Leary kindly came from Chicago to visit him.

Massachusetts General Hospital near Hart's home

After about two weeks, Hart told a reporter, "I'm all right now, but I've had a siege of it." Smith added, "Hart's appetite is excellent, he sleeps well, and will soon be able to sit up. The crisis is past, he is all right now, and you can bet your bottom dollar that he will win another race." Hart had lost eighteen pounds during his health scare. After three weeks of caring for him, Smith returned to New York City. Hart let Smith train fellow black pedestrian, Pegram, who was training for the 6th Astley Belt race.

FRANK HART.

The Pedestrianic Champion Rapidly Improving—Billy Pegram and the Astley Belt.

After a month of being struck by the illness, Hart was finally getting outside, taking carriage rides. He said, "My appetite is poor, owing to the fact that my stomach is very sensitive. I am able to get around my house pretty well, but I am very cautious. I do not expect to be able to go into training until late this fall. I am going to act with caution, and follow my physician's instruction, for I expect to have a few more trophies." It would be impossible for him to try to bring the Astley Belt back to America in September 1880 and the next O'Leary Belt challenge was postponed for several months to let him recover.

In October 1880, Hart severed ties with his agent, **Jacob Gottlob**, and planned to sail with O'Leary and others for England to support the American runners competing in the 6th Astley Belt race. However, while in New York City, he lost another child. On October 14, 1880, his baby son, **William Walter Hart**, eight months old, died of cholera, back in Boston and was buried in Woodlawn Cemetery. Hart decided to return to Boston and start training to defend the O'Leary Belt.

World Record Broken by Rowell

On November 5, 1880, **Charles Rowell** of England won the Astley Belt again and broke Hart's world record by one mile, reaching 566 miles. Losing the world record, especially to a Brit, was disappointing for Hart. Rowell won the belt by nearly 100 miles but went on to snag Hart's world record "for the fun of it." Hart publicly challenged Rowell to a six-day race in New York, saying, "I will put up dollar for dollar of his, and will beat him, and let him see that there is no fun in beating me."

The next O'Leary Belt was planned to be held during Christmas week, but Madison Square Garden had been condemned because of an accident on April 21, 1880, when the walls fell, tragically killing four people, two horses, and wounding sixteen other people. During the Hahnemann Hospital Fair, the front of the building facing Madison Avenue gave way and fell

Madison Square Garden Destruction

outwards, causing part of the roof to fall inside the building. "The cause of the accident was the dancing, which shook the beams and strained the trusses, causing one or more of the latter to give way." The builder of the building believed the roof gave way because of overheating of the timbers by gas.

Repairs had not been finished and the building could not yet be scheduled for December. But the American Institute Building (former Empire Skating Rink) was engaged for the race to be held in late January 1881, giving Hart another month of training.

The sporting world wondered if Hart would return to his previous dominance. "The impression in New York is that Hart is fearful of again entering in a long-distance match, or that having accumulated so much money he is not willing to again pound the sawdust."

Word spread, "It looks as if the young man from Haiti was breaking up." Was Hart washed up as an ultrarunner? "The general opinion among the pedestrian fancy is that Hart, the colored boy, has broken down. Hart should enter the (O'Leary Belt) race if only to prove to his friends that he is as game as ever and is not afraid to meet a number of good men."

CHAPTER THREE

Racial Hatred

John "Lepper" Hughes (1850-1921) of New York did not hide his racist hatred for Hart. He had been a "poor day laborer" before he found success in pedestrianism. He was born in Roscrea, Tipperary, Ireland, and was the son of a competitive runner. When he was a boy, he was a fast runner, won some races, and could run close to hounds in fox hunts. With no formal education, he emigrated to America in 1868 at the age of eighteen, became a citizen, and worked for the city of New York in Central Park. It was said that he was "stubborn as a government mule." He was called, "the Lepper" because of his peculiar way of walking with an odd jumping gait.

John Hughes

Daniel O'Leary and John Hughes

Hughes was known for his temper and often showed bad behavior in races. He desperately wanted to be recognized as the champion pedestrian of the world. It was reported, "Hughes is a boastful and ignorant fellow, with a fine physique and unlimited confidence in his powers." He had a deep personal hostility against fellow Irish American, **Daniel O'Leary,** who had beaten him soundly in the Second Astley Belt Race in 1878. Hughes blamed his backers for purposely poisoning his milk and swindling him out of all his prize money.

Since then, Hughes had experienced some success but had failed to win any of the big six-day races. His best six-day mark was 520 miles, when he finished sixth at the Rose Belt Race in 1879, won by Hart.

568 MILES AND 3 LAPS.

Hughes' Wonderful Record in the Six Days' Race

In the American Institute Building at New York.

But finally, on January 29, 1881, Hughes had the finest race of his career when he broke the six-day world record, achieving 568 miles in the "First O'Leary International Belt Race" held at the American Institute Building in New York City. Hart did not compete in the race, choosing instead to get ready to defend the original "American" O'Leary Belt, to be held the following month.

Hughes in International O'Leary Belt

As the Third O'Leary Belt approached, Hughes desperately wanted to win that O'Leary belt too and beat Hart in the process. He boasted that he would cover 600 miles.

Hart and Hughes Fight

In 1881, Bernard Wood's Gymnasium and Athletic Grounds on North 9th and 2nd Street (Wythe Ave) in Brooklyn, New York was a popular place for runners to train on an indoor sawdust track. In February 1881, both Hart and Hughes used the track to train for the upcoming O'Leary Belt. Hughes would often yell hate-filled racist slurs at Hart.

Hart had nothing good to say about Hughes.

One Sunday afternoon, while both were training there, they competed in an ego-based sprint together which Hughes won. Hart joked that at the upcoming match there would be no poison soup, referring to Hughes' excuse for losing the Second Astley Belt. He added that he would beat Hughes at the upcoming match.

"Hughes turned around and shouted, 'You lie, you black (n-word).' Saying this, he struck Hart with a powerful blow under the chin. Hart fell flat on his back but was up again in an instant and hit Hughes over the right eye." They continued to deliver blows, but Hart was no match for the bigger Hughes. Trainer Happy Jack Smith jumped in and separated them. "As Hart went away, Hughes shouted at him, 'I'll kill you the next time I meet you on the track." Hughes had a black eye, and Hart had a swollen cheek.

Frank Hart	John Hughes
Age: 24	Age: 30
Height: 5'7"	Height: 5'7"
Weight: 140	Weight: 150
Chest: 36	Chest: 42
Thigh: 19	Thigh: 19
Calf: 14	Calf: 13 ½
Shoe: 8	Shoe: 9

"LOW TRASH."

The Style of Animal Which Assumes the Title of Champion Pedestrian.

When a reporter asked Hughes why Hart didn't have a black eye, he replied disgustingly, "I would have had to put white marks on Hart to have given him black eyes, wouldn't I?" Hughes moved his training to the American Institute Building. His wife said, "He does not wish to associate any longer with such low trash as frequent the Williamsburg (Brooklyn) Gymnasium."

Third O'Leary Belt

The two bitter rivals competed in the Third O'Leary Belt six-day race held in Madison Square Garden with twenty starters on February 28, 1881, in front of 8,000 spectators. Hart was the heavy favorite among the betters. One said, "Hart will pump the life out of Hughes." Hart took the early lead. On the fourth lap, a Hart impersonator was spotted on the track and bounced by the referee, **Edward Plummer**. It was said he had been inserted on the track to rile up Hughes.

Hart was determined to stay ahead of Hughes. "Happy Jack Smith, his handler, who wears a fine diamond scarf pin, said that Hart, for the first time in his racing career, refused to obey his instructions. He

FRANK HART—JOHN HUGHES.

traveled altogether too fast in the first two hours of the race, keeping it up after repeated cautions to slow down. Jack ran around an entire lap with him to his endeavors to put on the brakes." Several "loafers" hung over the rails subjecting Hart to terrible racial insults, such as "You ought to be jerked from the track with a rope around your neck."

The Negro Hart Ill, and Finally Retires.

Unfortunately, Hart withdrew from the race due to nerve pain after running only 63 miles. The doctor reported, "He is suffering from intercostal neuralgia caused by taking cold during the walk wearing too light clothing." Bookmakers were not satisfied with the explanation, believing he quit to compete soon against Rowell who had come from England. Smith said, "The truth of the matter is, Hart tried to kill Hughes with the pace and succeeded in killing himself." Others speculated that his downfall was from his mode of living since he became rich and from his severe sickness the previous year.

Hughes was elated that Hart dropped out. He took the lead and reached 100 miles in 16:20, but he soon lost the lead when he went off track to take an alcohol bath. When he returned, he was stiff. "The change in Hughes' demeanor was marked. His stolid face had almost become a bright one when he learned of Hart's withdrawal, but now he scowled blackly at the new leader, and all the spirit seemed to have gone out of him. He couldn't or wouldn't run."

Hughes made frequent short stops on day two and experienced "excruciating pains in his stomach," causing him to fall on the track. He eventually got up but continued to complain loudly. "His face became pale and his whole body swayed to and fro like an intoxicated man." He finally quit the race after only 115 miles. "It was agreed that Hart and Hughes had allowed their personal animosity, by inciting them to an exhaustive struggle at the outset, to defeat them both. Both cried like babies and cursed their trainers, while their trainers as heartily cursed them back." Hart's public image took a huge hit, and criticism filled the newspapers. On his return to Boston, he said that he cared nothing for newspaper opinions.

To England

Hart sent in his deposit for the Seventh Astley Belt Race to be held in England, during June 1881, hoping to finally race against Rowell. He promised his friends that he would train hard and make a good account for  himself in the next race. On April 17, 1881, he sailed for England on the steamer *Canada* to get ready for the June race. His new manager, **John W. Luke**, a former private detective from New York City, went with him, along with one of Hart's black friends who would serve as his attendant. Night and day he trained running or walking on the deck of the steamer.

Happy Jack Smith did not accompany them. He had resigned as Hart's trainer because Hart would no longer train as Smith desired. After all that Smith had done for Hart, including nursing him back to health, their breakup was sad to see. He said Hart's downfall was from "cruising around town at nights when he out to have been in bed." Even during six-day races (12 hours per day), he would sneak out of his hotel without being seen by his trainer, dressed in "frills and fancy jersey" and party late into the night with friends. Smith, who was viewed as the best trainer in the sport, next became the trainer for **John** Dobler.

Hart arrived in England on May 1, 1881. He trained with **Blower Brown**, at Turnham Green, a public park in a suburb of London. As the race approached in June, probably because of over-training, his feet swelled, and his legs suffered from rheumatism. Unfortunately, he had to pull out of the Astley Belt race. He was bitterly disappointed. London sports reported, "Frank Hart, who came over here with the express intention of whipping all wobbling creation has gone in for rheumatism instead."

Hart went to Nice, France to get better. "He dabbled in horse racing and lost $10,000 on the turf in England and $5,000 in Paris. His trip cost him $17,000 (valued at $500,000 today, more than half of his fortune), and as he remarked in a resigned manner, 'It has cost many a man more.'"

Hart Arrested in England

FRANK HART ARRESTED

In London for Assaulting and Robbing a Woman.

Before returning to America, Hart got into trouble, was arrested, and charged with assaulting a French woman and stealing 30 shillings from her. The bail was set at £40, and a trial date was scheduled in London. It was reported, "It seems that Hart had gone with another black companion to a house of ill-fame and when the proprietress of the establishment ordered them away, they committed the alleged robbery of thirty shillings. The woman was afterward grossly assaulted as she pursued the flying pair to get them into custody."

Hart was caught, but his friend got away. A couple of weeks later, the Grand Jury threw out the case. *The London Age* reported, "The charge against Hart was utterly devoid of foundation and the grand jury without hesitation threw out the bill. Hart, leaving the court without a stain on his character." Unfortunately, this outcome was not printed in papers across America.

Hart returned in shame to Boston about a month later. He gave his side of the story to *The Boston Globe*, attempting to brush off the controversy of the original story that was published nationwide. He explained, "One evening, accompanied by a friend, I entered a bar room. There was a man and woman standing there, quarreling. The woman turned round to me and said, 'You have stolen thirty shillings which I just left on the counter.' At the same moment, the man said, 'You did. I saw you do it." I was aggravated and struck him. She then grabbed me by the throat, tearing the buttons off of my vest. I struck her and was at once taken to the Vine Street Police station, and in a few minutes released."

Another Daughter Born

On November 20, 1881, a daughter was born to the Harts, **Lillian Adelaide Hart** at their home on 8 Blossom, Ct. in Boston. Hart gave his birthplace as Haiti, West Indies, and his occupation as "Pedestrian" on the birth record. A year later they had another daughter, **Eugenie Adelaide Hart** (1882-1918).

Hart Attempts Comeback

Charles Rowell, the English champion, traveled to America to sight-see and Hart tried unsuccessfully to get him to accept a six-day challenge from him. He said, "I shall never be satisfied until I beat him." After nine months away from competition, in December 1881, he ran in a 75-hour exhibition race in Memphis Tennessee against legends, **Daniel O'Leary** (1846-1933), **Charles A. Harriman** (1853-1919), and **Henry Schmehl**

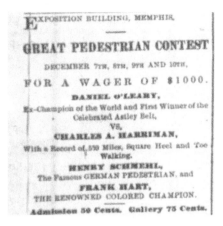

EXPOSITION BUILDING, MEMPHIS.

GREAT PEDESTRIAN CONTEST

DECEMBER 7TH, 8TH, 9TH AND 10TH,

FOR A WAGER OF $1000.

DANIEL O'LEARY,
Ex-Champion of the World and First Winner of the Celebrated Astley Belt,
VS.
CHARLES A. HARRIMAN,
With a Record of 550 Miles, Square Heel and Toe Walking.
HENRY SCHMEHL,
The Famous GERMAN PEDESTRIAN, and
FRANK HART,
THE RENOWNED COLORED CHAMPION.
Admission 50 Cents. Gallery 75 Cents.

(1851-1932). Hart won with 306 miles, the furthest he had raced in more than a year and a half.

With that tune-up, two weeks later, on December 26, 1881, Hart started in a six-day race put on by ultrarunner **John T. Ennis** (1842-1829) of Chicago, in the American Institute Building in New York City, with fourteen starters. Surprisingly, Hart was the favorite among wagerers. After two days, he reached an impressive 221 miles, just two miles behind the leader, **Patrick Fitzgerald** (1846-1900).

However, on the third day, Hart became sick from pleurisy (inflamed lungs) and quit the race after 229 miles, more than 40 miles behind – another failure. He said he had caught a cold during the previous race in Memphis. The race had billiard tables set up in the center area of the track and Hart spent most of the following days playing pool and watching the runners. Fitzgerald went on to win and break the world record with 582 miles.

The Diamond Whip Six-day Race

Hart went to New York City and set his sights on training in the American Institute Building for the next big six-day race to be held in Madison Square

Name.	Age.	Height.	Wt.	Chest.	Thigh.	Calf.	Shoe.
Rowell	28	5 6	136	36	23	15½	8
Noremac	24	5.3½	118	35	18	13	6
Panchot	40	5.5	138	33	17½	13	7
Fitzgerald	35	5 10½	115	42	22	16	12
Vint	36	5 7	127	36	18	12	5
Harnet	27	5 6½	132	37	18	13	7
Scott	38	5 9½	135	36		14½	8
Hughes	32	5 7	130	40	19	13½	9
Sullivan	27	5 6	130	37	19	14	6

Garden, the Diamond Whip, on February 27, 1882. This would finally be his chance to race against **Charles Rowell** who was undefeated in six-day races. But then came the shocking news that Hart's backers from former races refused to put up $1,000 for his entrance fee because of his recent failures. It was clear that his fortune was running out.

Frank Hart Not Admitted at the Eleventh Hour. The referee said he could enter anyway with agreement from all other entrants; however, they were not unanimous in letting him in without paying. He finally did raise the $1,000, with Rowell kindly contributing $100, but it was past the deadline. Again, some of the other entrants, including his nemesis Hughes, opposed his late entry. "Hughes positively refused to hear of Hart's admission on any terms." Hart was greatly disappointed, and his new backers tried hard to change Hughes' mind, but he refused. Hughes claimed that Hart owed him $100 and believed that if Hart was in the race, he would focus on preventing Hughes from winning, by dogging his steps.

Hart Allowed to Enter at the Last Moment. Within an hour before the start of the race, everyone was shocked to see Hart enter the Garden and head for one of the runners' cabins. The scorer at the great blackboard put up Hart's name. Reporters were informed that Hughes had finally consented to let Hart run. "The fact soon became known to the vast throng, and the cheers showed how great was the sympathy with Boston's colored athlete. Hart himself was overjoyed and was so moved that he could hardly speak." It turns out that the notorious police **Captain Alexander "Clubber" Williams** (1839-1917) convinced

Alexander Williams

Hughes to let Hart in – likely a little blackmail to pay off a shady favor Williams had previously performed for Hughes.

HART AND HUGHES.

"The Lepper" and the Colored Boy Not on Good Terms—The Former Hissed and the Latter Cheered.

At the start line, something surprising occurred. "Hart was chewing a toothpick, and as he turned, he saw Hughes. Stepping up to the latter, he grasped his hand and vigorously shook it." Early in the race, Hart ran alongside Rowell, which angered some in the crowd who speculated that Hart had been allowed to run to help Rowell. By running next to Rowell, he could also block other runners from passing. Hughes complained to the referee and wanted Hart to be kicked out of the race. The crowd "hissed" Hughes. Finally, some in the crowd screamed, "Clear the track, Hart," and he ran ahead. After Hart bumped Hughes while passing him, Hughes, shouted to the referee, "I rule this man out." Hart gave his side of the story to the referee and was allowed to continue. Whenever Hughes ran near Hart, a scowl would appear on his face.

BEGINNING THE LONG WALK

OPENING OF THE SIX DAYS' PE-DESTRIAN CONTEST.

On the first day, Rowell covered an astonishing 150 miles. Hart was in third place with 124 miles. Unfortunately, during the night, a cold settled in his chest and slowed him down the next morning. Gottlob, Hart's re-hired manager said that Hart began the race at the last minute with hardly any provisions, two bottles of ginger ale, and a bottle of cold soup and that his cabin was poor. But Hart continued and reached 217 miles after day two, 313 miles after day three, and 409 after day four, accomplishing the extremely rare 400+ miles in four days for the second time in his career.

Hughes broke down on day four, went at a "snail-like pace with an agonized countenance, a sorry figure on the track" and fell in the standings but recovered the next day. His remaining focus was to just beat Hart and the spectators cheered him on in his effort.

On the final day, Hughes kept gaining on Hart. During the final laps of the race, Hart, in one of his many colorful outfits, came up to pass Hughes, and he put out his hand for Hart to grasp. "The two bitter enemies were thus reconciled. Both raced like mad the length of a lap, and the crowd strained its lungs with shouting." But in the end, Hart prevailed and for the first time in nearly two years, he finished a six-day race. He placed fourth and reached 542 miles to Hughes' 535 miles.

The big story of the race was that **George Hazael** (1845-1911) of England became the first person in history to reach 600 miles in six days, crushing the world record and winning the diamond-studded whip. Hart won a much-needed, $1,500 (valued at $43,000 today) to maintain his lifestyle and pay off debts.

Hart Sued by Former Manager

At the end of the race, the referee was presented with a legal summons against Hart's winnings. His former trainer, **John W. Luke**, was suing Hart for $313.75, for lack of payment of services at the failed effort in England. Hart got wind of it and made his escape. "He put on a big overcoat and a high hat, fixed a huge cigar in his mouth, broke a hole in the roof of his quarters, climbed through, leaped ten feet to the ground, and got out the back door. There, a carriage awaited him and one of his backers thrust him into it, whispered to the driver, and saw him safely away." He went into hiding and was said to be dodging deputy sheriffs. Gottlob took control of Hart's winnings but could only get $1,000 from race management who held back $500 to satisfy Luke's claim. Hart's reputation in Boston took another blow.

Hart Leaves Boston with Financial Difficulties

At the end of March 1882, *The Boston Globe* reported, "Frank Hart has left Boston for good. He says he hasn't a friend in the city, either white or colored." Hart was being pursued by other debtors. Some of Hart's land

and buildings in Boston on Blossom Street were seized by the Sheriff and put up for auction to cover his foreclosed mortgage. (The Wyndham Boston Beacon Hill Hotel stands there today). His wife still lived on some property a block to the west on North Anderson Street.

Hart went on a southern barnstorming tour to Tennessee and Arkansas, with O'Leary and others, where he competed in leisurely races and exhibitions, more for money, less for competition. He was pleased to be away from controversy and treated like a celebrity again.

GREAT RACE of the CHAMPIONS

SKATING RINK.

Commencing Tuesday Evening, April 11, 1882. Grand 100 Hours Pedestrian Tourney.

DAN O'LEARY, ex-Champion of the World.
JOHN DOBLER, Holder of the 75-hour Champion Belt.
FRANK HART (colored), Winner of the O'Leary Belt and Long-distance Champion of America.
J. L. DOWNEY, Champion of Louisiana,
PAT DALE, of New Orleans, and
HART'S UNKNOWN.

Don't Fail to See the Start for the Lead.

In June 1882, with money back in his pocket, Hart returned to Boston, entertained at The Casino, raced on foot against cyclists in handicapped races, and made other circus-like appearances at carnivals.

Casino Police Gazette Diamond Belt Six-Day Race

At the end of July 1882, Hart competed in a serious six-day race with several of the famous pedestrians of the time, including his nemesis, Hughes. The race was held in the massive Casino Building in Back Bay, Boston, "The crowd was very small, and in the immense building looked even less than it really was. Hughes made fifty miles and then drew out

Start of Casino Race. Hart and Hughes on right

in disgust. He gave as his reason that the track was not good, being soft in places." But the real reason likely was because Hughes had not been training much, showed up with "considerable surplus flesh," and clearly did not like running with Hart.

Hart ran 125 miles during the first day and established a large lead which he held throughout the race, winning with 527 miles – his sixth six-day race victory. He won the Police Gazette Belt, his third major belt. "One thing is very certain, that Hart has in a measure redeemed himself with many of his old friends who had lost faith in him, owing to his late failures on the track. Hart, after fortune smiled on him, neglected himself so much as to cause no confidence to be placed in his foot powers. He seemed determined to win back his lost laurels and again take the front rank in pedestrianism." In the *Boston Globe*, he graciously thanked all those involved at the Casino for their kindness to him during the race. At age 25, perhaps he was maturing or had a good public relations person helping him. It is unknown if he was taking care of his family with three young children.

Championship of the World Six-day Race

WALKING MATCH.

Another Great Tramp Begun at the Madison Square Garden.

The next major race was the "Championship of the World" six-day race at Madison Square Garden on October 23, 1882. Hart wisely kept a low profile and seemed to concentrate on serious training. He had reunited with world-class trainer, Happy Jack Smith. Hart said, "Happy Jack Smith and I have buried the hatchet and I am confident of breaking all past records." Smith was very pleased with Hart's conditioning going into the race. Hart reembraced Boston and said that he was representing the city and would bring back the colors to the "Hub."

NAMES.	Date of Race.	First Day. M. Y.	Second Day. M. Y.	Third Day. M. Y.	Fourth Day. M. Y.	Fifth Day. M. Y.	Sixth Day. M. Y.	Total. M. Y.	Hours off track.	Average miles per hour.
Hazael	March 4, '82	135 170	105 440	102 220	91 440	106 660	60 50	600 220	34 6 25	6½
Fitzgerald	Dec. 24, '81	121 1,165	101 1,705	104 1,705	102	92	60	582 55	23 30 31	4.91
Vint	May 26, '81	133	100	101 220	94 880	92 660	57 600	578 605	28 44 39	5 10
Hughes	Jan. 24, '81	134 449	94 1,540	96 1,320	91 440	83	68 440	568 825	25 50 00	4.89
Rowell	Nov. 1, '80	146 1,509	102 1,035	91 1,005	76	76 251	73 1,572	566 63	32 38 38	5.18
Hart	April 10, '80	131 165	94 221	93 665	86 1,595	86 1,505	73 165	565 165	23 23 09	4.77
Noremac	Dec. 24, '81	110	97 985	84 1,495	105 1,320	106 1,540	60 495	565 494	25 07 39	4.83
Herty	Dec. 31, '81	119 880	86 660	109	56 1,485	89 715	55	556 275	20 59 35	....

Previous bests by competitors

When the nine runners came to the start line, Hart looked the most impressive in his red drawers, gray trunks, white shirt, and fancy jockey cap. Hughes was in the race and swore to run "the n-word" down on the first day. After the start, the two went out hot and finished the first mile in 6:16. It was observed, "Hart is the prettiest ped on the track. His gait and the earnestness with which he jogs along are inspiring much confidence in his being, perhaps, the dark horse."

Hughes took the lead and was the first to reach 100 miles in a very speedy 14 hours. (The world record stood at 13:26:30 set by Charles Rowell at the Diamond Whip race earlier in the year). Hart ran well but there still was some drama involving him. While Smith was sleeping, Hart drank champagne, something Smith did not want him to do.

All of the Nine Peds Still Keeping the Track.

THE SCORE AT 3 A. M.

	M.	L.
HUGHES	157	4
ROWELL	144	7
HART	141	7
HAZAEL	141	3
FITZGERALD	132	0
HERTY	128	3
NOREMAC	127	1
PANCHOT	125	1
VINT	103	0

THE SCORE AT 3 P. M.

	M.	L.
FITZGERALD	489	0
NOREMAC	472	0
HERTY	459	0
HUGHES	453	0
HART	439	0
VINT	415	0

On day four, Smith was frustrated with Hart who was still 30 miles behind the leader Fitzgerald. He said, "He is lazy. You can't depend on him at all. If a man won't do as you tell him to, he puts you in a hole. When we give Frank beef tea, he spurts it on the track. He wants nothing but slops all the time. I never saw him so before. He's playing possum with you all the time." In protest, Smith temporarily quit as Hart's handler during the afternoon. Hart worked harder and surpassed 400 miles in four days as did four others. It truly was a world-class race, although the world record holder, Hazael dropped out with 383 miles.

On the morning of day five, Hart fell on the floor of his room with terrible cramps. Smith, who had returned, worked on him, and he soon recovered. Then Hart apologized to Smith for the way he treated him the previous day and promised to follow his advice for the rest of the race. He pulled ahead of Hughes and reached 476 miles at the end of the day.

FITZGERALD THE WINNER.

THE CLOSE OF A WALK THAT WAS NOT ALTOGETHER SUCCESSFUL.

Very Little Money Left Above Expenses to Divide Among the Pedestrians—Receipts from Admissions Less than $20,000.

On the final morning, Hart sat in a chair with a badly swollen knee. He said, "I have honestly done my best, although everyone has called me lazy. But the truth is the atmosphere (smoke) of the Garden would kill anyone. Here I am now, as you see me, played out." He tried to continue but withdrew at 10 a.m. with 482 miles. In the end, **Patrick Fitzgerald** from Long Island won with 577 miles. Smith again stopped training Hart and eventually moved on to train Fitzgerald.

Boston considered Hart's effort a failure. There were some rumors that Hart had been bribed to quit, but he vigorously denied that. It was reported, "The next six-day race will be his last, when he hopes to return to Boston, having reclaimed his lost laurels." Would he really retire? No, it was a proven source of enormous income for him. But Hart just wasn't keeping up with the competition. Since Hart set the six-day world record of 565 miles in 1880, nine others had

Six-day Personal Bests as of 1883
1. George Hazael 600
2. James Albert 588
3. Patrick Fitzgerald 582
4. Dan Burns 578
5. Robert Vint 578
6. John Sullivan 569
7. John Hughes 568
8. George Noremac 567
9. Charles Rowell 566
10. **Frank Hart 565**

surpassed his mark during the next four years. He was now ranked tenth in the world.

Hughes vs Hart Fiasco

Early in 1883, again desperate for money, Hart issued Hughes a challenge to race for 26 hours, and Hughes accepted. A promoter took up the event and scheduled it for March 1883 in a minor venue in Troy, New York, across the Hudson River from Albany. A few years earlier, female pedestrian events were held in that industrial city. They should have realized that this was a very bad idea to get the two hated rivals together. Throughout the race, the two had confrontations and were said to be in "a quarrelsome mood."

HUGHES HAS A ROW WITH HART.
Breaking Up a Walking Match with the Colored Man in Troy.

Late into the race, Hughes was partaking a bit too much of stimulating booze. He had a good lead, 142 miles to 121 miles, but then he went crazy. He accused his backers of cheating him. He yelled, "You sold me out before, and you have done it again. The (n-word) has been sleeping, but his score was going up all the time while I was doing honest work." Hart responded by punching him in the face and a "lively fight occurred for a few minutes until the crowd separated them." The police came and found Hughes bleeding from his nose. The hall was cleared, and they put an end to the match. Hughes only earned $3.05 from the match. The manager, Gilbert, tried to skip out of town without paying the bills but was found. He lost $200.

Another Fight in Baltimore

The Hart and Hughes disgusting feud continued two months later in June 1883, during the Fox Diamond Belt six-day race at Kernan's Summer Garden in Baltimore, Maryland.

Kernan's Summer Garden.

3,947 PEOPLE WITNESS THE START
of the
SIX DAYS' INTERNATIONAL WALK
for the
CHAMPIONSHIP OF THE WORLD.

ALBERT, NOREMAC, HUGHES, HART
and twelve others now on the Track,
IN ONE OF THE MOST SPIRITED CONTESTS
Ever Witnessed in this Country.
Beautiful Garden.   Fifth Regiment Band.
Admission 25 cents.   ‡

Hughes, who was leading the race on day four with 410 miles, accused Hart of conspiring with **George Noremac** (1852-1922) to try to run Hughes off the track. Hart denied it and called Hughes names. Hughes struck Hart, pounding him in the face and throwing him over the rail, and "a lively tussle" continued. "Mrs. Hughes, who has been a faithful attendant on her husband, interfered to separate the men. Hart tried to bite her but only succeeded in biting the sleeve of her dress. The combatants were parted." The police stopped the fight. Hart treated his black eye, changed his ripped shirt, and continued, but only reached 400 miles, not enough to be eligible for any winnings. Hughes went on to win with 558 miles.

Frank Hart's Early Races

Date	City	Place	Miles	Place	Notes
Apr 25-26, 1879	Boston, MA	Music Hall	119	1	30 hour. $100
May 14, 1879	Lowell, MA	Huntington Hall	50	1	50-miler 8:50
May 21, 1879	Boston, MA	Mammoth Tent	39	2	Beanpot, $45
May 26-31, 1879	Boston, MA	Mammoth Tent	424	1	six-day, Interstate, $150
Jul 23-26, 1879	Boston, MA	Music Hall	263	2	75-hour 3 day, $150
Sep 8-13, 1879	Providence, RI	Park Garden	363	1	six-day, Champion Belt, $300
Sep 22-28, 1879	New York City, NY	Madison Square Garden	450	4	six-day, 5th Astley Belt, $3,750
Oct 22, 1879	Long Island, NY	Frunell's Athletic Park	61	3	12 hour race, $12.60
Nov 24-29, 1879	Newark, NJ	Newark Rink	373	1	six-day, 12 hours per day, $500
Dec 22-27, 1879	New York City	Madison Square Garden	540	1	six-day, Rose Belt, $3,000
Apr 5-10, 1880	New York City	Madison Square Garden	565	1	six-day, 2nd O'Leary Belt, WR, $21,567
Feb 28-Mar 5, 1881	New York City	Madison Square Garden	63	DNF	six-day, 3rd O'Leary Belt, quit 1st day
Dec 7-10, 1881	Memphis, TN	Exposistion Building	306	1	75 Hours
Dec 26-31, 1881	New York City	American Institute	229	DNF	six-day, quit on 3rd day
Feb 27-Mar 4, 1882	New York City	Madison Square Garden	542	4	six-day, Diamond Whip, $1,500
Apr 11-14, 1882	Nashville, TN	Rink	268	1	100-hour race
Apr 24-29, 1882	Memphis, TN	Exposition Building	425	1	123-hour race
May 12-15, 1882	Little Rock, AR	Alexander Park Hall		DNF	Four-day race
Jun 23-24, 1882	Springfield, MA	The Rink	127	2	26-hour race
Jul 31-Aug 5, 1882	Boston, MA	Casino to Five	527	1	six-day, Police Gazette Diamond Belt
Oct 23-29, 1882	New York City	Madison Square Garden	482	5	six-day, World Championship
Mar 17, 1883	Troy, New York	Hall	121		26-hour race
May 28-Jun 2, 1883	Baltimore, MD	Kernan's Monumental Th	400	4	six-day, Fox Diamond Belt
Jun 27-29, 1883	Fall River, MA	Forest Hill Gardens			5 hours each night

53

CHAPTER FOUR

Ex-Champion

Frank Hart's life in 1883 was at a low point. He had blown through his riches and his reputation as a professional pedestrian was tarnished. He was viewed as being hot-headed, undisciplined, and a womanizer. His wife and children were no longer being mentioned as being a part of his life and by then were likely gone. Many people had tried to help him, even his original mentor, Daniel O'Leary, who called him "ungrateful." Trainers did not last long working with him. Hart was no longer referred to by the flattering title of "Black Dan." Certainly, some of the criticism against him was due to racial stereotypes, which he fought hard against. He wanted to regain the glory and fame he had felt in previous years.

PEDESTRIANISM.

Frank Hart and the $500 Diamond Ring— Stories of the Parties Involved.

To make things worse, he had a young woman, **Frances "Fanny" C. Nixon**, arrested, accusing her of stealing a diamond ring from him valued at $526. The press was quick to point out that a black man was accusing a white woman, unheard of at the time. She had met him at his 1880 world record race at Madison Square Garden and they developed a relationship. He claimed that the night before he left for England in 1881, she had stolen the ring from his vest pocket. She countered that he had given it to her as a gift before he left. She admitted that she later sold it to a pawnbroker for $250. The court released her on bail and apparently the case was soon dismissed.

California Here Hart Comes

On November 8, 1883, Hart left Boston to travel to California for the first time. Money in pedestrian contests was becoming harder to find and it was hoped that the West Coast would deliver. He was invited to compete in a six-day race in San Francisco with O'Leary, and two Californians, **Charles**

MECHANICS' PAVILION.
NOVEMBER 19TH TO 24TH,
Great Four-cornered Pedestrian Tournament
DANIEL O'LEARY AND FRANK HART
....AGAINST....
C. A. HARRIMAN and PETER McINTYRE.
$2,000 A SIDE AND GATE MONEY.
ADMISSION, 50 CENTS.
☞ Doors open at 7 P. M. SUNDAY NIGHT. ☜
Musical Festival To-night (Sunday)
from 8 to 12,
By the Entire Second Regiment Band.

A. Harriman, and **Peter McIntyre**, in what was called a "four-cornered" match. The East Coast team's miles would go against the West Coast team. Perhaps because of Hart's known aggressive conduct in races, a rule was put in against any "hustle, push, impedance, or interruption with any other contestant."

Hart Gives a False Background

Hart received a great reception in California and became an instant celebrity. San Francisco wrote, "Hart, the negro pedestrian, is coming to this city. He will be given a reception by the colored people." He was met at the ferry landing by a band and escorted to the *Pacific Life* newspaper rooms where he was given a banquet.

But Hart, wanting even more attention, characterized himself as a wealthy lawyer. An article was printed stating that he was a member of the Boston Bar. "Owing to an unfortunate stutter, Hart is a poor pleader, but his opinions on legal matters are so sought for that he is able to hire a pleader to present his ideas in court." *The Boston Globe* was surprised by the lawyer news and implied that it was fiction. He also stretched the truth of his recent six-day accomplishments, claiming that he held the current world record.

The New York *Sportsman* got wind of Hart's "lawyer profession" claim and a correction was later printed in a San Francisco newspaper. The New York editor wrote, "Hart may be a great lawyer – we have never heard him plead for other than a release from a creditor. Before reading the story of Hart's great ability as a lawyer, we thought his fame rested chiefly on his reputation as a pedestrian and a masher (a man who chases after women)."

California Four-Cornered Six-day Race

The San Francisco Four-Cornered race began right after midnight on Nov 21, 1883, in Mechanics' Pavilion. At the end of day four, the match was tight. Hart had a one-mile lead with 370 miles and his team score with O'Leary led by only five miles.

Mechanics' Pavilion

A gossip paper wrote, "Hart has nearly all the time from two to a half-dozen while female visitors in his tent, and on the track, he is the frequent recipient of loral offering from the fair sex. One lady tossed him a bunch of violets as he was walking by, which he did not see. She, thinking herself slighted, brought about an explanation and the little affair terminated happily, the parties becoming fast friends."

Hart reached 500 miles for both the individual and team win. The miles achieved were lower than expected. A critic wrote, "O'Leary (475 miles) would probably have done better had he paid more attention to the number of miles he should have covered, instead of watching the door and gate money." The event was financially successful for Hart. He stayed in California, challenging people for matches and putting on exhibitions at carnivals.

Muldoon's Great Six-Day Race

William A. Muldoon (1845-1933) was a Greco-Roman Wrestling Champion who won the world championship in 1880. Starting in 1883, he toured America promoting athletic events. In early 1884, he announced that he was going to sponsor a "Great Six Day Race" in San Francisco's Mechanics' Pavilion. Runners could win a prize package of $2,000. To

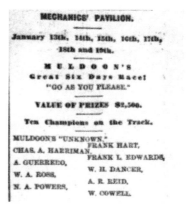

make the event even more interesting he announced that he would have a mystery runner in the race (Muldoon's Unknown) who would compete against Hart. The identity of the runner would not be revealed until race day, but wagers could be made on his Unknown. The great pedestrian promoter and sportswriter, **Fred J. Englehardt**, who helped Hart get his start in the sport and cross the racial barrier, was the manager of the event.

The race started on January 14, 1884, with ten starters. **John Dobler** turned out to be the Muldoon's "Unknown." Despite all the marketing, attendance was rather poor. Hart reached 100 miles in 19:45 and was in first place with 115 miles on the first day. "The gas was turned down low, and the band in attendance was composed of so few pieces as to hardly fill the hall from end to end with the sound of music." Dobler became stiff and sore and fell well behind. "The Unknown is not only unknown but rapidly becoming invisible."

THE WALKERS.

Hart and Harriman Are Still in the Lead.

On Day four, Hart had a sore toe and planned to have the toenail "amputated," and lost the lead to **Charles A. Harriman.** On the final day, the race was very close with an exciting finish. With three hours to go, Hart pushed ahead and won with 487 miles, only two miles ahead of Harriman. Hart had again won in California and was presented with a gold-headed cane.

California Fame Exhibitions

Now a California celebrity, Hart started to tour around the state. He competed in a 10-mile bike race where he was characterized as an "expert cyclist." He only lasted seven miles. Next, he rode in a 26-mile bicycle race at the Mechanics' Pavilion. "This colored

MECHANICS' PAVILION.

GREAT 26-HOURS BICYCLE RACE.

Commencing at 9 P. M., February 21st, and ending at 11 P. M., February 22d.

JOHN S. PRINCE of Boston, Champion of America.
H. W. HIGHAM of Nottingham, Champion of England.
T. W. ECK of Toronto, Champion of Canada.
LOUISE ARMAINDO of Chicago, Champion Lady Bicyclist of the World.
FRANK H. HART of Boston, Champion Pedestrian, also expert Bicyclist.

champion pedestrian spun around the track doubled up in such a manner as to indicate that the third vertebrae of his spine had dropped out." He reached 169 miles, in last place, and said he would stick to traveling on foot.

Hart left California and headed back east to get ready for the next big race in Madison Square Garden at the end of April 1884. After two weeks, people were puzzled why he hadn't arrived yet and assumed that he was training on the way back. Hart's New York friends had sent Hart $175 to pay for his expenses to travel back from California and they too didn't know what was going on. He was assigned a hut for the race but was a no-show as the start approached. In this race, **Patrick Fitzgerald** broke the world record with 610 miles.

Colored Baseball?

Where was Hart? It turned out that he stopped in Denver, Colorado to put together a lucrative match to be held there later in the month. He sent word to the New York race management that he was in Chicago and had joined a semi-pro "colored" baseball team. He claimed that he was hired to play shortstop on the Black Stockings in St. Louis, Missouri. The claim that he played for this team is very much in doubt.

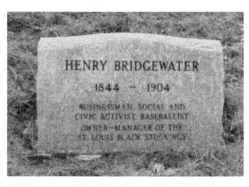

The Black Stockings were owned and managed by **Harry Bridgewater** (1844-1904) who had been born into slavery and became one of the most influential and wealthiest black businessmen in St. Louis. He had a goal of organizing a national black baseball league, but it never came together during his lifetime. Bridgewater evidently had recruited Hart to play for him. It seemed that Hart had played briefly in 1883 for the Boston Vendome Hotel Black Baseball Club, and for Saratoga Springs' Leonidas Black Baseball Club, so he had some baseball experience.

While Bridgewater was putting together the baseball team and season, Hart was still competing as a professional ultrarunner. A six-day heel-toe walking match was held in Denver Colorado, at Belmont & Hanson's Rink, for him to compete against **William Edwards** an experienced pedestrian from Australia. Edwards won 426 miles to Hart's 416 miles.

William Edwards

Hart never played for the St. Louis Black Stockings and instead continued in professional pedestrianism. There was no mention of him being on the team as the season took place during the summer and fall of 1884, as they were competing for the championship. Instead, he was away, very busy, running in races. Also, he never was a baseball player in the Negro Baseball League, as some have claimed. That league was not formed until 1920.

Six-day Brawl in Chicago

On July 7, 1884, Hart competed in a six-day match in Chicago put on by O'Leary, at the Battery D. Armory. It turned out to be a terrible fiasco. Hart quit the race after 58 miles, claiming that he was not being scored fairly. His nemesis, Hughes, later went on a tirade, causing a "free-for-all-fight" on the track. The police had to break it up. Pedestrian **Daniel Burns** (1860-1914),

BATTERY D ARMORY ON THE LAKE FRONT

of Elmira New York, was sent to jail and Hart was given 24 hours to leave the city.

Even though he was leading, Hughes quit the race claiming that it was fixed, and the scores were not being properly recorded. He asserted that he was assaulted by **George Noremac** and that Hughes' wife and child were assaulted as he was being driven from the track.

O'Leary denounced Hughes' statement as a lie. "He said Hughes was a chronic kicker and had been barred from walking matches all over the country. He started the fight and two of his friends tried to help him, and they were arrested." The race went on because O'Leary paid bonuses to those who stuck it out. "Financially the match was a fizzle" because it competed with the Democratic National Convention in town.

THE SCORERS.

In August 1884, Hart put on a 25-mile exhibition in Springfield, Ohio, but was "deeply disgusted" because only a dozen spectators came out. He quit after only going 12 miles. "Many thought him a counterfeit of the genuine Hart, but he walked enough to show that he was a professional."

The Bizarre Memphis Fraud Race

During the fall of 1884, Hart traveled in the Midwest, trying to drum up running matches, without much success. He next went south to Memphis, Tennessee for a 124-hour match held in the Exposition Building on December 22, 1884. A man named **George Tidy**, of England**,** arranged the event. Hart, **Daniel Burns**, and **Gus Guerrero** of California started. It turned out that Tidy was a fraud and skipped out as the runners were on their second day. He left debts behind of nearly $400. "Hart, Guerrero, and Burns are all still in

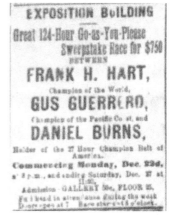

the city and are not to blame for Tidy's ugly work. They are very anxious to see him themselves."

First Six-Day Roller Skating Race

During 1885, there were only a handful of six-day races held. Hart looked for other endurance sports to win money. In February 1885, a six-day roller skating tournament was announced to be held March 2-8, 1885, at Madison Square Garden under the management of **William Wood**, the secretary of the New York Athletic club.

Champion skaters signed up to compete, and the field included some other pedestrians. The winner would receive $500, and a diamond belt valued at $250. The event turned out to be an embarrassment for Hart. "Very few of the contestants appeared in good training and Frank Hart, the pedestrian seemed almost unused to the skates. He lifts

his skates as if they were snowshoes and seems to imagine that all he has to do is put his foot on the floor and he will go ahead." After ten hours he was dead last with only 29 miles.

"THE ELMIRA NEWSBOY."

Death of the Champion Long-Distance Roller Skater.

But he kept trying. Late on the first day, it was reported, "He was crawling around the track, reminding one of a 16-year-old maiden, making her first venture as a roller skater, if by any stretch of the imagination the dark-skinned runner and his soiled corduroy suit can be thought of in the same sentence with a 16-year-old maiden in a rinking costume." His skating gait was so odd that the other skaters gave him a wide berth when they came near. He finally quit on day two after 123 miles. His old trainer, **Happy Jack Smith** handled **William Donovan**, age 18, the eventual winner with 1,092 miles. Sadly, Donovan died only a month after his victory due to exhaustion and pneumonia.

Hart's Lifestyle

In 1885, it was reported that Hart had squandered $50,000 that he had earned over the past five years. That was worth $1.5 million today. He seemed to never have a home and likely lived in posh hotels as he traveled around the country. In November, Hart returned to Boston after being away for 2.5 years. Clearly, he had abandoned his family, who were still living there. His loyalty to Boston had wavered. In one race he listed his residence as Bradford, Pennsylvania.

Barnstorming Pennsylvania in 1886

After participating in several 1885 races in the New York area and winning little money, it was announced that for the next year, he had allied with **Charles A. Harriman,** called the "Harriman and Hart Pedestrian team." They were an interesting pair, Hart was "short and thick," and Harriman was "tall and slender." They planned to barnstorm Pennsylvania in 1886, go to California, and then on a 3–4-year trip to Australia.

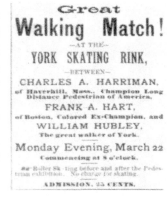

Great
Walking Match!
—AT THE—
YORK SKATING RINK,
—BETWEEN—
CHARLES A. HARRIMAN,
of Haverhill, Mass., Champion Long
Distance Pedestrian of America.
FRANK A. HART,
of Boston, Colored Ex-Champion, and
WILLIAM HUBLEY,
The great walker of York.
Monday Evening, March 22
Commencing at 8 o'clock.
Roller Skating before and after the Pedestrian exhibition. No charge for skating.
ADMISSION, 25 CENTS.

HART BARRED OUT.
He is Not Allowed to Start in a Seventy-five-Hour Match.

Things got off to a rough start. In January 1886, at Elmira, New York, they were barred from a race because fellow veteran pedestrians refused to let them start. The objection seemed to be because of their alliance, and the potential for shady tactics.

For the next few months in 1886, they competed in several 75-hour races in cities across Pennsylvania. With this three-day format, they could do a race every other week, rather than once-a-month six-day races. It was all about trying to make a lucrative living. But still, running over 200 miles in each of those races took a toll. So, they next put on weekly 51-hour races, covering over 150 miles. Hart certainly was piling up the 100+ mile finishes, with about 35 thus far in his career.

Charles Harriman

But these Pennsylvania races had problems because of dishonest managers who didn't pay bills, and at times they were boring events for spectators, watching worn-out runners. After one race it was written, "All parties were disgusted with the contest." Hart's reputation was no longer great. He was referred to as "Ex-Champion." The alliance with Harriman only lasted about four months and by June 1886, the Pennsylvania barnstorming tour ended.

Failure in New Bedford

Hart disappeared from the sport for several months, visited Hawaii, but reappeared in October 1886, "grown heavy." He competed in his first six-day match in over two years, a 12-hour-per-day race in New Bedford, Massachusetts. He was focused on placing high enough to earn winnings, but on day five, after 280 miles, he quit. "His trainer followed with an anxious face and the audience soon learned that he would not return. His face has been haggard and his step feeble the last 24 hours. Stretched upon a cot in his tent covered with heavy blankets, he said, 'I'm gone. I'm done for. There is no use in my keeping on. I know I cannot take a place.'"

Hart Organizes His First Race

Since it seemed like Hart couldn't win money in races anymore, he decided to go into the race-organizing business. His first was a six-day, 12-hours per day, 72-hour race, put on at the Columbia Skating Rink in Boston on November 1, 1886. The race went well, but Hart quit after 205 miles because of bowel issues. **Gus Guerrero** won with 404 miles.

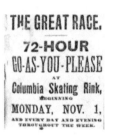

THE GREAT RACE,
72-HOUR
GO-AS-YOU-PLEASE
AT
Columbia Skating Rink,
BEGINNING
MONDAY, NOV. 1,
AND EVERY DAY AND EVENING
THROUGHOUT THE WEEK.

Hart Arrested, Freed and Flees Boston

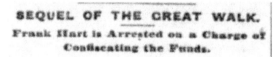

SEQUEL OF THE GREAT WALK.

Frank Hart is Arrested on a Charge of Confiscating the Funds.

Hart's greed and lack of business sense got him into big trouble. After the race, he was charged with confiscating funds from **Edward E. Grant** (1845-1888), who served as the manager of the race. The top four finishers had been promised a share of the gate money but received nothing. The day after the race, Hart was stunned when he was arrested in front of his hotel. He said, "All the money I received from Grant yesterday was $637.38, out of which I paid the band $90 and **Bose Cobb** (rink owner) $133.12, leaving $414.20 for me to account for." He stated Grant and others wanted to exclude him from the profits. He said, "This is my reason for keeping the money, as I am not going to be played for a fool any longer."

The biggest problem was that Hart was supposed to share the profits with the top finishers of the event, and he did not. He was held by police for an hour, but it was determined that the matter was for a civil court, not a criminal court. After he was released, he said that he was determined to keep the money. He quickly left Boston and was criticized in the press for "leaving the walkers in a rather poor financial condition." His reputation in the sport took yet another big hit.

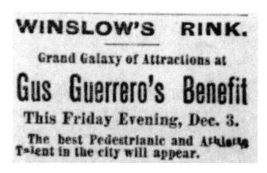

Gus Guerrero

The Boston public was appalled by Hart's despicable greed and behavior. He had finally burned bridges with his hometown. A "grand benefit" was organized for the race winner, **Gus Guerrero**, to raise deserved money for him that Hart had run off with. The evening event full of running exhibitions was well attended and a great success. A month later, it was reported, "Frank Hart, who is called the lazy colored pedestrian says he will enter legal proceedings against a Boston paper for publishing his portrait and placarding him as a thief." He threatened to sue for $20,000 and started to claim Fall River, Massachusetts as his home. He resented being called lazy, especially by men who had never tried to run hundreds of miles.

Philadelphia Diamond Belt Six-Day Race

In late February 1887, Hart, now age 30, competed at a huge six-day race in Philadelphia, Pennsylvania with most of the greatest ultrarunners of that time, even **Gus Guerrero**, whom Hart had recently swindled. **John Hughes**, Hart's racist nemesis, was also there.

"Hughes harangued the crowd and said all he wanted was fair play. He kept up his ill temper until near the starting time. Then he went outside the building and did not return."

Hart still had speed and completed the first mile in first, in 6:10, but Guerrero soon overtook him. In this highly competitive race, after day one, Hart was in fourth place with 103 miles, and after day two in second with 201 miles. He finally had a good race again and held onto second place after day three with 289 miles and 367 miles after day four. On day five it was reported, "Hart is still the freshest man on the tanbark and his walk is without the slightest trace of a limp."

The Twelve O'Clock Score.			
Miles. Laps.		Miles. Laps.	
Robert Vint...300		6 Wm. Burrell...205	9
Frank Hart...289		5 Peter Golden...204	11
Anton Strokel...281		5 Alex. Miller...203	1
Peter Panchot 270		John Dillon...204	
D. Bennett...268		3 Sam Day...187	10
C.D. Noreman 263		Alf. Newhart...178	2
James Albert 241		J. C. Adams...161	2
Alfred Elson...236		5 sergt. Kramer 130	5
Geo. Tilly...207		5	

In the end, Hart finished in second place with 518 miles, twelve miles behind **Robert Vint** (1846-1917), an Irish-American and shoemaker from Brooklyn, New York. Hart won a much-needed, $2,000, but he was a sore loser. "Hart is a little disgusted at not winning first money and claims it was the fault of his trainer, who would not allow him to cover enough ground the first two days."

Robert Vint

VINT THE WINNER.

ENDING THE SIX DAYS' RACE WITH TWELVE MILES' LEAD.

HART GETS SECOND PLACE

The building was jammed when the final results were announced, and the police worked to shove the crowd into the rear center of the floor. "They were still pushing men out of the way when one of the large rafters holding the floor up from the cellar broke with a noise something like that of a muffled cannon and the floor began to sink. The officers were the first to run and a regular panic ensued, the crowd shoving and knocking each other down in their attempts to get away from the spot. Quiet was finally restored and the floor fell no further. No one was severely injured."

Hart Organizes Another Race

DENOUNCES HART.

The Pedestrian's Trainer Wants His Money.

Hart competed successfully in Nebraska and after a win was given a huge reception. His reputation was improving until he organized a six-day match against Harriman in Oshkosh, Wisconsin in September 1887. Hart was up to his old tricks again. "**W. A. Gregg**, who officiated as Hart's trainer claims Hart skipped out Sunday without paying his bills, among them being one due Gregg for his services. Gregg said that last spring after a six-day race in Boston, he skipped out with all the gate receipts, and all people ought to be warned against Hart."

In November, at a highly competitive six-day race in Philadelphia, Hart tried to keep up with the new ultrarunning sensation, **George Littlewood** (1859-1912) of England. On day

one, Hart burned himself out and had to drop out after 118 miles. Littlewood won with an amazing 569 miles.

Hart closed out 1887 by disappointing Lancaster, Pennsylvania, in not showing up for their race. He sent a letter letting them know that he was ill, but that was a lie. Instead, he competed that same week in a more lucrative race in Kansas City, Missouri where he placed second with 429 miles.

1888 International Go-As-You-Please

In February 1888, Hart competed in another historic international six-day race held at Madison Square Garden with 47 starters, put on by **Frank W. Hall**. The field included five athletes of color, Hart, **Edward Williams**, **Merritt Stout**, "the Arabian," a painter from New York City, **William Burrell**, of Chicago, and **Fields**. Hart was no longer a feared champion but still respected as one to watch out for. At the start, the old building, planned for demolishment, was packed "as full as a sausage case," with about 12,000 people. Hart was dressed in a blue shirt, red trunks, gray tights, and an old, checkered jockey cap.

A spectator bridge had been constructed over the track for those who wanted access to the infield that contained a lemonade booth and a newspaper stand. Other attractions were knife-throwing boards, baseball targets, cane racks, and places to buy railroad sandwiches, sawdust pie, soda water, popcorn, candy, fruit, and a bar with 100 bartenders dealing out beer. Cries of "'Drop a nickel in the slot' caught the people curious of their own weight, their lifting powers and the strength of their lungs, and those who were partial to tutti-frutti chewing gum"

There were 150 scorers hired for shifts. Callers shouted out the number of the runner as they passed under a wire, identified by a black card on their chest. There were mistakes with so many runners. Hughes, as usual, complained that he had been short-changed two miles. Others, including Hart, stopped at the scorers' stand to protest strongly. The scorers, led by **Edward Plummer**, threatened to quit if they were not left alone, and not allowed to take breakfast breaks.

THE START.

A fight occurred on the first day and for once, Hughes and Hart were not involved. **Robert Vint** didn't like **John Dempsey**, a boxer, dogging his heels and hitting them. "Vint got a blow in the mouth from Dempsey's fist bringing blood. Dempsey called Vint a name which he didn't take kindly to." Vint dislocated his thumb from a punch.

Another disruption occurred on the track. "Policeman Creighton essayed to suppress a one-legged boy of fourteen years, but the cripple refused to leave the path of the men and when the policeman attempted to take him out of the Garden, the boy fought him using his crutch for a weapon. The rebellious lad was locked up."

Hart covered 75 miles in 12 hours, 130 miles after 24 hours, and 226 miles on day two. "Frank Hart, the 'cheerful colored boy,' was the cleanest and most unconcerned of the twenty men left on the track. He was in no hurry but kept going." He reached 313 miles on day three, and 393 miles on day four in fifth place. He still had a constant, rapid, upright walk. In the end, he reached a very remarkable 546 miles for fourth place.

621 MILES.

Albert Breaks the World's Record.

James Albert (1856-1912), from Philadelphia, Pennsylvania, broke the six-day world record with 621 miles. Hart had now witnessed the breaking of the world record five times. In this race, eight men went over 525 miles.

Hart won about $2,500. "Frank Hart was a badly used-up winner. He was hoarse and trembling. He denies that he was lazy and says that no lazy man would ever go into the six-day business. He is to leave it and expects to be appointed a Philadelphia policeman or go into the business there. Hart once made a fortune as a champion walker but enjoyed life too well to keep it."

THE FINAL SCORE.		
	Miles.	Yards.
ALBERT	621	1320
HERTY	583	600
GUERRERO	564	
HART	546	660
GOLDEN	538	880
MOORE	531	1320
STROKEL	526	880
NOREMAC	525	440
DILLON	504	1320

WALKERS ANGRY AT HALL.

THEY CLAIM THAT HE HAS NOT TREATED THEM WITH FAIRNESS.

He and others believed strongly that they had been cheated by the race manager, Hall, taking too much profit, something Hart had previously done himself and thus he had no room to complain. He said, "There isn't the ghost of a doubt that crooked work was done." He was so upset that he swore that he would never enter another race.

Frank Hart's Races 1883-1888

Date	City	Place	Miles	Place	Notes
Sep 10-15, 1883	Baltimore, MD	Kernan's Monumental Th	417	1	
Oct 19, 1883	Holyoke, MA	Front Street Rink	35	DNF	with women
Nov 21-26, 1883	San Francisco, CA	Mechanics's Pavilion	500	1	six day, Pacific Slope Championship
Jan 14-19, 1884	San Francisco, CA	Mechanics's Pavilion	487	1	Muldoon's Great Six Days Race
Mar 12, 1884	Los Angeles, CA	Turn Verein Hall	25	1	25-mile walking exhibition, 8:27:30
May 19-24, 1884	Denver, CO	Belmont & Hanson's Rin	416	2	match against Edward Williams
Jul 7-12, 1884	Chicago, IL	Battery D Armory	58	DNF	DNF in protest over scoring
Jun 8-13, 1885	Baltimore, MD	Kernan's Monumental Theatre		DNF	quit on 4th day
Aug 1885	Paterson, NJ	Little Coney Island Cours	48		50-mile walking record attempt
Aug 17-22, 1885	Paterson, NJ	Little Coney Island Course			
Oct 5-10, 1885	Binghamton, NY		207		75 hours race
Oct 28-31, 1885	Scranton, PA	Lackawanna Rink	234	4	75 hours race
Feb 10-12, 1886	Williamsport, PA	Keystone Rink	251	2	75 hour race
Mar 1-5, 1886	Cincinnati, OH	Queen City Rink			six-day
Mar 22-25, 1886	York, PA	York Skating Rink			match against Harriman
Apr 8-9, 1886	Scranton, PA	Arcadian Rink			51-hour race
Apr 16-17, 1886	Bradford, PA	Parlor Rink	265	1	75 hour race
Apr 26-27, 1886	Carbondale, PA	Metropolitan Rink	183	1	51-hour race
Aug 2-7, 1886	Paterson, NJ	Little Coney Island	>319	1	12 hours per day
Oct 4-9, 1886	New Bedford, MA	Bandcroft Rink	280	DNF	quit on day five
Oct 21-23, 1886	Pittston, PA	West Pittston Rink	136+		75-hour race
Nov 1-5, 1886	Boston, MA	Columbia Rink	205		six day, 12 hours per day
Jan 5-9, 1887	Utica, NY	Lafayette Rink	245	3	heel-toe
Feb 20-25, 1887	Philadelphia, PA	Elite Rink	518	2	six-day, $2,000
Mar 14-15, 1887	Jackson, MI	Assembly Opera House	>96		50-hour match
Apr 2, 1887	Jackson, MI	Assembly Opera House	15	1	15-mile walking match, 2:22:26
May 2-7, 1887	Philadelphia, PA	Elite Rink	485	4	six-day
May 18-21, 1887	Lincoln, NE	Funke's Opera House	199	2	50-hour race
Jun 6-11, 1887	Omaha, NE	Exposistion Building	400	1	six days
Sep 19-24, 1887	Oshkosh, WI	Casino Rink			Duel match with Harriman
Oct 10-15, 1887	Philadelphia, PA	Columbia Rink	376	1	six day, 12 hours per day
Oct 19-21, 1887	New Bedford, MA	Adelphi Rink			75-hour race
Nov 21-26, 1887	Philadelphia, PA	Elite Rink	118	DNF	quit on day two
Dec 26-31, 1887	Kansas City, MO		429	2	six-day
Feb 6-11, 1888	New York City, NY	Madison Square Garden	546	4	six-days, $2,500

CHAPTER FIVE

Declining Running Career

O'Brien's Six-Day Race

Hart's retirement did not last long. He entered the next big international six-day race held on May 7, 1888, in Madison Square Garden. For this race, 96 men entered and 44 started. One rejected runner claimed he could go 750 miles.

In this race was, **George Littlewood** (1859-1912) of Sheffield England, the world record holder for <u>walking</u> 531 miles in six days, reached 100 miles in less than 16 hours. After the first day, Hart was already more than 20 miles behind. Unfortunately, on the morning of day two, after running 122 miles, in seventh place, Hart was said to look lazy and quit the race as he was falling in the standings. He realized that he would not finish in the money. Littlewood went on to win with 611 miles.

George Littlewood

Throughout 1888, Hart competed in several 75-hour races in New York, Connecticut, Delaware, and Pennsylvania, winning most of them, but earning less than hoped for. Feeling rejected by Boston, he now claimed to be from Philadelphia, Pennsylvania.

Fox Diamond Belt Six-Day Race

Hart competed in the most historic six-day race in history, held November 26-December 1, 1888, in Madison Square Garden. There were 100 race entries but only 40 starters were approved. It was put on by **Richard Kyle Fox** (1846-1922), editor and publisher of the sporting publication, *The Police Gazette*.

THE LAST GREAT CONTEST ON THE TANBARK.

Leading up to the race, Hart trained at the Polo Grounds in Upper Manhattan each day "under the watchful eyes of trainers and admirers" with several other entrants, including Littlewood.

It would be the last six-day race held in the original Madison Square Garden, previously called Gilmore's Garden, and P.T. Barnum's Hippodrome, made from an old train depot. The old building would start to be demolished on August 7, 1889. It was located on the block that currently holds the New York Life Building.

Nearly 10,000 people filled the building for the start with 37 contestants. Through the first night, it became obvious why the building needed to be replaced. "The ring in the center of the garden looked as if it had been swept by a hurricane. Booths were overturned and the floor was flooded with melted snow, which had dropped through the crevices in the roof." It didn't seem to bother Littlewood, who covered 77.4 miles in the first 12 hours.

Hart was about 12 miles behind and struggled early. "Several doses of bug juice were taken, and the Haitian youth was wobbly in the legs, and his eyes rolled in a fine frenzy for some hours." He covered 113 miles on day one, in 11th place. Again, racist comments were made by reporters that he was being lazy. But later he received compliments. "Hart, the colored man, seemed to grow more graceful in his

movements as the other stiffened in their limbs." He reached 204 miles after 48 hours and had moved up to 9th place. A total of ten men had reached 200 miles during the first two days, which had never been accomplished before in one race.

By the beginning of day three, only 18 of the 37 starters were still in the race. Littlewood seemed to be the greatest eater among them. During the morning he ate eleven lamb chops, washing them down with two large bowls of oatmeal gruel. Littlewood was being handled by Hart's former trainer, **Happy Jack Smith**. Hart reached 283 miles after day three. He confined himself to a fast walk instead of trying to run or do a dog trot.

Littlewood took the lead during the early morning of day four, close to world-record pace. During the afternoon of day five, he reached 500 miles. Hart continued to have a good race but was 70 miles behind in seventh place. Smith put together a pacing schedule for Littlewood to make sure that he would break the world record and earn a $1,000 bonus. He needed to average better than four miles per hour.

George Littlewood

At 7 a.m. on day six, with 563 miles, Littlewood caught up to the world-record pace. "The contingent of British subjects, which had infested the Garden since the race began, cheered and the sleepers in the back seats awakened and joined in the applause while the band played 'Rule

Britannia.'" Hart was about 80 miles behind but still working hard to get in the money.

THE RECORD IS BROKEN.

Littlewood, the Sheffield Pedestrian, Does Some Great Work.

On the final day, Hart passed 500 miles at 10 a.m. Littlewood passed 600 miles at 3 p.m. He went on to break the world record with 623 miles. As typical with six-day races of the era, they were actually scheduled for 142 hours, so the crowds could get home before Sunday. Littlewood stopped at 8:07 p.m. and later came out for one more mile at 9:27 p.m. At 10 p.m., he was presented to the crowd as the champion of the world, and then he made a victory lap wearing the diamond belt.

Hart finished in sixth place with 539 miles, running a smart race. He won $463 for his week's effort. Ten men exceeded 500 miles. Hart had now witnessed the six-day world record broken for the sixth time. They all thought that it would soon be broken again, but it would stand for 96 years until Yiannis Kouros broke it in 1984 with 635 miles.

World International Six-day Race

On Feb 6, 1889, Hart left for California on the *Cincinnati Express* with other runners to participate in a six-day race there. They arrived in San Francisco a week later greeted by a crowd of fans eager to catch glimpses of them. A six-day race was put on by **Frank Hall** in Mechanics' Pavilion. He hired many people to serve as ushers, bartenders, and scorers. Contestants needed to reach 525 miles to get a share of the gate receipts.

Hart badmouthed the former world record holder **James Albert**, of Philadelphia, Pennsylvania, who chose not to travel to California to compete in the race. He said, "Jim Albert is a coward. He could not run in the company that is in this city now and so he wanted a sure thing of getting $1,000 from Frank Hall before he came here. Because he did not get it, he raises a fuss and tries to injure the race."

The race began on Thursday, February 21, 1889, at 10 p.m. in the Mechanic's Pavilion. California six-day races typically did not have a problem racing across Sundays. "So great was the jam of a great crowd gathered at the entrance that the managers decided to throw open the doors two hours ahead of the advertised time. Then there was a frantic rush for the seats of vantage." 12,000 people were on hand for the start of the 28 runners. The pace was torrid. The bands in the galleries and on the main floor had not finished their first piece before the second mile was reached by the front-runners, including Hart.

As usual, there were complaints about the scoring early on. Hart and others threatened to quit the race if they didn't score the runners correctly.

Hart reached 100 miles in 17:40 and then took the lead in the race. He completed 131 miles in 24 hours, which was a Pacific Coast record. "The colored waiters collected in a body and danced a breakdown 'patting juba' and using their platters for tambourines."

Hart reached a very impressive 221 miles after 48 hours. (The world record at the time was 257 miles held by **Charles Rowell**). He led the procession, and at times singled out **Edward C. Moore** (1860-1927), of New York, "as a victim for his old trick of dogging following him as the shadow pursues the substance. He seems to have a set purpose of irritating the rival to whom he pays his attention."

Moore and Hart, Substance and Shadow.

On the second night, "Hart looked tired and dozed as he walked. From time to time, he roused himself, rubbed his eyes and the back of his head, and hastened his speed with springing steps." At the end of day three, Hart reached 297 miles and was behind **Thomas Howarth** (1860-1932), of Ratcliffe, England, by three miles.

Band members amused themselves by putting facial decorations such as whiskers on sleeping spectators and then using their instruments to rouse their victims with great laughter. "A wad of blazing paper in close proximity to a sleeper's legs and a yell of 'fire' proved a favorite method until officials put a stop to it with threats of arrest for arson." They then resorted to pouring ice-cold soda on the sleepers.

MECHANICS' PAVILION.

SIX	TO-NIGHT!
SIX	TO-NIGHT!
SIX	THE DAY'S SENSATION.
SIX	WORLD'S INTERNATIONAL
DAYS	WORLD'S INTERNATIONAL
DAYS	RACE.
DAYS	
GO AS	MECHANICS' PAVILION.
GO AS	MECHANICS' PAVILION.
GO AS	ALL THE CHAMPIONS
YOU	A most exciting struggle for the
YOU	supremacy. Moore, Howarth and
PLEASE	Hart, the leaders of the hotly-con-
PLEASE	tested fight, are all up together and
PLEASE	making the most remarkable time
PLEASE	on record. A number of dark horses
RACE	coming to the front.
RACE	GREAT 10-MILE RACE.
RACE	CARTWRIGHT and GUERRERO.
RACE	The two Champions will run a 10-
RACE	mile Race TO-NIGHT at 10 o'clock
RACE	for a purse of $100 and a $500 side-
RACE	bet.
RACE	MUSIC BY GOLDEN GATE MILI-
RACE	TARY BAND.
RACE	Admission, 25 and 50 cents.

SAWDUST TRAMP NEWS.

Another Breezy Day With the Lunatics at the Pavilion

The race manager. Hall walked on the track alongside Hart for a while and was accused of coaching him. When Hart dogged Howarth's pace, things got testy. "Finally, when Howarth was on the verge of madness, he turned on his tormentor and hotly accused him of trying to spike him. Hart replied with equal warmth and the two fought with their jaws for half a dozen laps. They were about to come to blows at one time, but interference prevented a slogging match, and the cloud of war blew over."

Because of all his dogging, Hart was given the title of "the bloodhound of the sawdust path."

Hart was very demanding with his trainer **Frank Edwards**. He once demanded Malaga grapes and declared he would not run another mile without grapes. "California was able to supply a bunch or two, even at such an unreasonable season, and after eating half a dozen off a bunch, the cranky tramp imagined that he was in fine spirits and spurted for four or five miles at a seven-an-hour clip, eating fried egg sandwiches as he traveled." He finished day four with 359 miles, just one mile behind Moore. On day five Hart had a sore knee and it was bandaged. He reached 436 miles, still within striking distance for the win.

Hart took the lead on the final day. The firm track was taking its toll on him. His trainer said, "The tanbark has been very hard. It was not fine enough, and there was too much on the track. There was no spring to it, no give to it. As a consequence, it used up the men's feet in a horrible way. We had to put our man's foot in a mold of plaster of Paris and used everything we could think of to reduce the swelling." There was a lot of doubt whether Hart or anyone would reach the 525 miles required for prize money. Hart reached 500 miles with 6.5 hours to go.

Hart went on to win in a very close race in front of 13,000 people. "The most demonstrative applauders were the representatives of the colored population who were present in force to cheer their champion in his victory." With fifteen minutes to go, Moore reached 525 miles and quit. Hart, only six laps ahead, also stopped. His win earned him a huge payoff of $3,720. It made his California trip worth it if he could just not squander the money away.

The next day he was asked how he felt. He said, "I'm as hungry as a bear. I have been a professional pedestrian for twelve years and I never suffered so much in my feet and limbs as I did during the match just finished. The track was a poor one. The heat from it caused all the walkers' feet to be parboiled." When asked about his plans, he said, "I intend to stay right where I am. California is good enough for me. I am going to open a sports saloon in this city. Californians have treated me well so far, and I think they will in the future." He quickly opened a saloon at 3 Morton Street, which he called "The Strand." The street was known as the "sleaziest street in town," later renamed, "Maiden Lane."

Another Six-day Race in San Francisco

With the financial success of the February race, another one was quickly scheduled for May 1889. Hart and others trained every morning in downtown San Francisco on an outdoor track, 19 laps to a mile, in a large open space in the back of the old St. Ignatius Building on Market Street. "Later in the day a few of them would take a run through Golden Gate Park to Ocean Beach and back again,

6 DAYS AND 6 NIGHTS

6 DAYS GO-AS-YOU-PLEASE RACE!
6 DAYS MECHANICS' PAVILION,
6 DAYS MAY 9TH to 15TH.
6 DAYS ——THE EVENT OF AMERICA :——
6 DAYS $2,500 in Prizes!
6 DAYS In addition to the gate money to be
6 DAYS given to the winner.
6 DAYS The entries to date are as follows:
6 DAYS James Alberts, record 621.
6 DAYS Dan Harty, record 605.
6 DAYS Gus Guerrero, record 591.
6 DAYS Bobby Vint, record 579.
RACE Frank Hart, record 566.
RACE E. C. Moore, record 554.
RACE Tom Howarth, record 551.
RACE Old Sport Campana, record 550.
RACE Peter McIntyre, record 525.
RACE Frank Edwards, record 500.
RACE Jerry Taylor, record 460.
RACE W. H. Scott, record 500.
RACE And many others.
RACE Entries now open to all. Privileges for
RACE sale. Address FRANK HALL, Central
RACE Park, Eighth and Market streets.

finishing the day's work by another two hours spin on the track. In this way, the different peds do from 30-50 miles a day."

James Albert

There was continued bad blood between Hart and Albert who came west to race. Albert had said some nasty things about Hart to the press and Hart vowed to beat him in the upcoming race soundly. Hart would have to eat his words. Albert reached 142 miles in the first 24 hours and won convincingly with 533 miles. Hart quit on the third day, with 203 miles "footsore, sick, and disheartened."

The San Francisco Chronicle quickly turned against Hart and wrote, "Frank Hart is disgusted with the race. He came here expecting to be the winner. Champion Albert's appearance at the outset frightened Hart and becoming weak-hearted, he pulled out of the contest." There probably was truth to that, because the night after Hart quit, he ran a 10-mile sideshow race with no problem. There were only a few hundred spectators at Albert's finish.

California was quickly losing interest in the six-day races. Hart's perceived California six-day gold mine was drying up.

Return from California

After participating in some more minor races on the West Coast, without earning any significant money, Hart gave up on California. In December 1889, he headed for Cleveland, Ohio, where he did poorly in a six-day race.

He stated plans to head to Australia, a claim he had been making for years. In April 1890, he stated at a six-day race in Pittsburgh, Pennsylvania, that it would be his last appearance on an American track. "He intends to locate in Australia and has already one or two good pedestrian engagements booked for there." But as the race began, Hart started to complain about his feet. He said if he didn't place in the money, he would cancel his Australian tour, apparently needing the money to get there. He quit after the first day with only 77 miles. His Australian plans were off. He continued to race in the eastern states, but he would always quit early if it looked like he would not win any money or if the crowds were small. His motivation to compete was only to win money.

In September 1890, in Detroit, Michigan, Hart, age 34, finally had another good six-day race, his first in more than 18 months. He covered 100 miles in 17:11 and 123 miles in 24 hours, leading 27 runners. He continued running well, with 218 after 48 hours, and 288 miles after three days. "Hart runs as though the track were India rubber."

THE BROWN BOY AHEAD.

Frank Hart in the Lead in the Go-as-You-Please Race.

He slowed in the final days, lost the lead at times, but in the end, won with 479 miles, just one further than Moore. He only put in enough effort to reach the 475-mile milestone to qualify for winnings, about $780. For the rest of 1890, he continued to travel trying mostly unsuccessfully to arrange races that would earn him money.

Hart's New Home - Minneapolis, Minnesota

He competed in another six-day, 12-hours per day race in Jan 1891, at Minneapolis, Minnesota, and was very popular there. "Hart was the center of interest for all the colored people present, of which there were a great number." Unfortunately, with sore feet and a swollen knee, again out of the money, he quit after 48 hours. He liked the attention received and decided to make Minneapolis his home for several years. He was still referred to as "the colored boy," even though he was 35 years old. They did say he looked much younger than his age, but it was a typical racist label for the era.

First Six-day Race in Madison Square Garden II

In March 1891, the first six-day race was held in the new Madison Square Garden II, located on the same block as the old one that was demolished. It had been open for nearly a year. An outer track, ten laps to a mile, was constructed for the runners along with an inner track to be used by other athletic attractions. The race was highly competitive with 36 starters. After the first day, Hart, about 30 miles behind the leader, reached 100 miles and quit the race. **John Hughes** went on to win with 558 miles.

Madison Square Garden

SIX DAYS' TRAMP.

The Great Tanbark Walking Match in Madison Square Garden is Well Under Way.

The next month, Hart made a rare return to Boston for a six-day, 72-hour race. It was observed, "Frank Hart, the veteran, colored pedestrian, did not seem to be in the best condition and acted rather tired." He was out on the first day. He estimated that he had career earnings and wager winnings totaling $100,000 during his 12-year career (valued at $3.2 million today) and that he had hardly anything to show for it. He said that it went out just about as fast as it came in. The four valuable belts that he won during the height of his running career had all been won away from him, something that saddened him greatly.

1,000-mile Race in St. Paul

In 1891, Hart, still with a home base in Minnesota, took on a wager for a 1,000-mile race against **Henry O. Messier**, (1862-1945) of Milwaukee, an experienced six-day runner, for a $1,000 wager. The race would be for ten hours per day and estimated that it would go for 23 days. The only available building in Saint Paul was in a basement under Mussetter's Drug Store on Grand

St. Paul, Minnesota

Avenue block. A tiny track was constructed, 27 laps to a mile. The first man to reach 1,000 miles would be the winner. Hart was very confident and said he would wager all the money he had that he would cover the distance at least three hours ahead of Messier. They started on May 14, 1891. The race was a huge bust, lost by Hart. After 244 miles, and six days, about 21 miles behind Messier, Hart quit, claiming that his feet were so sore that he could not continue. He lost a bundle of money.

Legacy

At the end of 1891, Hart cared more about his legacy. He started to embellish stories for the press. He claimed that he used to be a steel engraver that worked in the National steel engraving bureau during President Ulysses S. Grant's first administration (1869-1873). That was likely fictional because he was a grocery clerk in Boston during that time. He also stated that he had been in more six-day, go-as-you-please races (25) than any other man living. Nobody at the time kept track. **George Noremac**, **Samuel Day**, and probably a few others had him beaten by a long margin. He also claimed that he broke the six-day world record twice, but only did it once.

St. Louis Six-Day Race

At a six-day race held in St. Louis, Missouri, Dec 21-26, 1891, Hart's wife was mentioned as attending a race for the first time. "Hart, the colored boy, is the freshest man on the track, but he is notoriously lazy. His pretty wife sits up in the balcony all day long watching him." It is  possible that the lady was indeed his wife, who came to visit him, sharing some news about his family.

THE GO-AS-YOU-PLEASE.

The Pedestrians Are a Bit Weary, but Most of Them Are Still in the Ring.

Hart ran hard in this race, trying to prove he still had championship ability. "Hart is surprising his most ardent admirers. He is one of the most decidedly dangerous men in the race, and if he only keeps up courage and avoids becoming lazy, he will surely finish near the top of the list." He reached 110 miles on the first day. Unfortunately, after 280 miles, on day four while in second place, he quit because of blistered feet.

Hart's Son Becomes a Runner

Hart did have some contact with his family. He learned that his son, **Frank S. Hart**, age 14, had started participating in running races. This was true, later in 1894, a mention was made in the *Boston Globe* that Frank Jr. won a two-mile foot race that was part of a massive picnic of 2,500 "colored people" held at Highland Lake Grove, south of Boston. The article confirmed that he was the "son of the walker."

Quitting Races Early

In 1892 at the age of 35, Hart seemed to change his racing strategy. Instead of going out hard to win at all costs, he had a more patient attitude. At a six-day race in Kansas City, it was written, "Frank Hart, the colored champion, glides along steadily at an easy dog trot. He says it is not his style of a race exactly, but he will be around in the vicinity of the leaders at the finish." Unfortunately, his old attitude came back when he dropped out at 132 miles because he saw no chance to win.

Observers felt that Hart was "going downhill" as a runner and he indeed had a string of six races where he had quit early. It was speculated, "These long walks not only bring physical wreck but frequently permanent mental disorder." His pattern of quitting before the six days ended continued in New Orleans in February 1892 when he quit with 215 miles "probably finding that the task of obtaining a position in the race was too severe for the reward in sight." It had been more than a year since he had finished a six-day race all the way to the end. In most of those races, he could later find the strength to earn $25 by racing in a side-show 10-miler while the rest of the six-day runners continued plodding along. Quitting early was his new reputation.

THE CHAMPION WON.

HOAGLAND FINISHED FIVE MILES AHEAD OF FRANK HART.

In April 1892, Hart finally finished a six-day, 12 hours per day, heel-toe walking race to the end, in his adopted hometown of Minneapolis. During the race, he did a little "trash-talking" and said that **Willard Alonzo Hoagland** (1862-1936) of Auburn, New York, was not as fast as people had been saying he was. This bugged Hoagland, and he had the last laugh, winning the race with 315 miles, five miles ahead of Hart. A rumor circulated that Hart had gone insane after the race finished. But the next day he was seen on the streets, laughed, and said, "Well, I haven't reached that stage yet."

Willard Hoagland

When pedestrians were offended by another, they typically would issue a challenge for a duel, not with pistols, but with their feet. Hoagland issued a challenge to Hart for a ten-mile heel-toe walking race and would give Hart a half-mile head-start. Both deposited $100 each in a bank to accept the duel. As with most of these duels, it never took place.

A CELVFR FAKE.

A Girl Walker Proved a He—Engeldrum a Sure Winner.

On May 16-21, 1892, Hart competed in a six-day race at the Jackson Street Rink in Saint Paul, Minnesota. On the evening of the fourth day, a pretty, blonde-haired woman, named Eva, came in and issued a challenge to run against professional pedestrian Aggie Harvey and any other women in an exhibition race. The side-show race was arranged and the amateur beat Harvey by a lap. Harvey wanted a rematch, so the next evening, it was repeated, and Eva lost by three laps in front of a crowd of 500 spectators. "Eva went up to Frank Hart to explain that her corset had been laced too lightly and that she could not run well, when Hart detecting something 'mannish' in Eva's manner, made a grab for the wig and taking it off, exposed a head of hair which only a man could wear." She admitted that she was a man. It was discovered that he was a porter in a nearby hotel. "The makeup was perfect, and the young man carried himself like a real woman, carrying on a handkerchief flirtation with some of the male spectators in the most approved style, and fooling even the best of them." Hart finished with 329 miles, in third place.

The Battery D Six-Day Race in Chicago

After five months away from racing, Hart appeared at a five-day race in Chicago, Illinois on October 18, 1892, at the Battery D Armory with 18 starters on a small track, sixteen laps to a mile. Hart, age 38, was not washed up yet. He reached 128 miles on the first day and 199 miles in 48 hours. He came away with his first win in over two years, reaching 479 miles. But the race was a failure among the spectators. By mid-race, only 200 people watched at any one time.

Health Scare in Wisconsin

A month later in November 1892, he participated in a six-day, four hours per day race in Racine, Wisconsin. An alarming report was issued, "Hart went to pieces on the track last evening and his career as a pedestrian is no doubt closed. He was taking with hemorrhage of the lungs." After only 62 miles, he was vomiting up large clots of blood in front of hundreds of people. He was able to board a train for Chicago to get treatment. Newspapers across the country were reporting that "he will never be seen on the track again." Rumors spread that he was near death in a Chicago hospital, but then his friend reported that he was going to race the following month in St. Louis, Missouri.

Frank Hart's Races 1888-1892

Date	City	Place	Miles	Place	Notes
Mar 9-10, 1888	Birmingham, CT	Tingue Rink		DNF	DNF
Mar 30-21, 1888	Fair Haven, CT	Quinnipiac Rink	>100	1	won, $75
Apr 9-14, 1888	Denver, CO	Mammoth Rink	473	1	six-day
May 7-12, 1888	New York City, NY	Madison Square Garden	122	DNF	six, days, quit day two
May 19, 1888	New York City, NY	Recreation Hall	124	2	24-hour race
Jun 1-2, 1888	Ansonia, CT		134	1	27-hour race
Aug 9-11, 1888	Troy, New York		292	1	75 hour race
Oct 3-6, 1888	Willmington, DE	Wilmington Rink	216	1	75 hour race, $160
Oct 18-20, 1888	Philadelphia, PA	Elite Rink	279	1	$80
Nov 26-Dec 1, 1888	New York City	Madison Square Garden	539	6	six-day. $463, Littlewood WR
Dec 24-29, 1888	Pittsburgh, PA	London Theater	86		
Jan 10-12, 1889	Fair Haven, CT	Quinnipiac Rink		DNF	50-hour race, DNF
Jan 30-Feb 1, 1889	Bangor, ME	Norombega Hall	104	3	27-hour race, 20 laps to a mile, $25
Feb 22-17, 1889	San Francisco, CA	Mechanics' Pavilion	525	1	six-day, $3,720
Mar 21-23, 1889	San Jose, CA	Horticultural Hall	148	2	32-hour match, 8 hours per day
May 10-15, 1889	San Francisco, CA	Mechanics' Pavilion	203	DNF	Quit on third day
Jun 12-15, 1889	Santa Cruz, CA	Pavilion	180	2	four days, four hours per day
Oct 21-26, 1889	Tacoma, WA	Alpha Opera House	150	2	four days, four hours per day
Nov 9, 1889	Victoria, BC		10		ten mile mach against Ed Shade
Dec 23-28, 1889	Cleveland, OH		>131		
Jan 1, 1890	Pittsburgh, PA	London Theater	11	DNF	12 hour exhibition, quit very early
Feb 24-Mar 1, 1890	Detroit, MI	Detroit Rink	106	DNF	Quit on day two
Apr 7-12, 1890	Pittsburgh, PA	Grand Central Rink	77	DNF	Quit on day one
May 21-24, 1890	Chicago, IL	Second Regiment Armory		DNF	75-hour race, quit on day one
Sep 2-7, 1890	Detroit, MI	Detroit Rink	479	1	six-day, $780
Oct 15-18, 1890	Altoona, PA	Emerald Hall	258	3	72-hour race
Jan 26-Jan 31, 1891	Minneapolis, MN	Washington Rink	186	DNF	quit day four, swollen knee
Feb 24-Mar 1, 1891	St. Paul, MN	Lowry Arcade	378	2	six-day, 12 hours per day, $370
Mar 16-21-1891	New York City	Madison Square Garden	100	DNF	Quit after day one
Apr 15-18, 1891	Boston, MA	Winslow's Rink	68	DNF	Quit on the first day
May 15-20, 1891	St. Paul, MN	Mussetter's Drug Store	244	DNF	1,000 mile race, ten hours per day
Jun 8-13, 1891	Denver, CO	Coliseum Hall	>100	DNF	Cancelled early for poor attendance
Aug 10-19, 1891	Minneapolis, MN	Shade's Park	94	6	six day, four hours per day
Sep 29-Oct 4, 1891	Elmira, NY	Madison Ave Square	238		
Dec 21-26, 1891	St. Louis, MO	Natatorum	280	DNF	Quit day four, blisters
Jan 13-18, 1892	Kansas City, MO	Vineyard's Hall	132	DNF	12.5 hours per day, quit on day three
Feb 22-27, 1892	New Orleans, LA	Washington Artillery Hal	215	DNF	Quit on day four, out of the money
Apr 25-30, 1892	Minneapolis, MN	Panorama Building	310	2	12 hours per day, $250
May 17-22, 1892	St. Paul, MN	Jackson St. Rink		3	12 hours per day
Oct 17-22, 1892	Chicago, IL	Second Regiment Armor	479	1	five-day
Nov 21-25, 1892	Racine, WI	Belle City Hall	62	DNF	six day, four hours per day, blood

CHAPTER SIX

Final Years

frankHart
Colored Champion

By late 1892, many of the original six-day professional pedestrians had left the sport, using their winnings to establish other careers, some of them pursuing illegal activities. Running professionally had been part of his life for fourteen years. At the age of 36, now referred to as an "old pedestrian," Hart was determined to continue to compete and prove his doubters wrong.

St. Louis Six-Day Race

Hart recovered and showed up in St. Louis for Professor Clark's Six-day Tournament held on December 19-24, 1892, at the Natatorium (swimming and gymnasium hall). People were astonished to see him a week before the race. "Frank Hart, the famous colored ped arrived in the city yesterday, a living contradiction to the rumors that had been circulated about his ill health. He denies that he coughed up a

St. Louis, Missouri

lung and part of his liver." He trained with other competitors at the Natatorium and was seen reeling off mile after mile. He indeed started the race and looked good in the field of fifteen runners. "A new lease of life appears to have been meted out to the old-time colored pedestrian."

HART LOSES HIS HEAD.

The Well Know Negro Pedestrian Acts in a Peculiar Manner During a Contest.

Hart reached 100 miles on the first day but then another alarming health scare took place. "He acted like a maniac while covering the last mile but returned to sensibility and resumed the race." He had picked up a stool-bottom chair which was at the edge of the track, walked in front of the music stand, and threw it at the pianist with all his might. The musician dodged it, and the police came quickly. "They knew Hart had no reason in the world for acting as he did and thought he had gone daft. Hart emphasized this feeling himself by yelling more than a dozen times in a perfect frenzy, 'You want to run a man crazy!' He was finally pacified and resumed his journey around the ring."

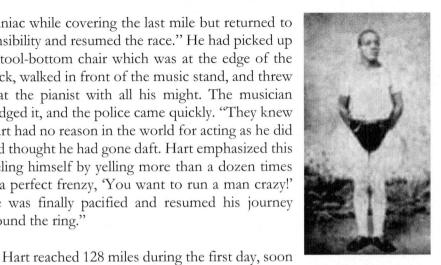

Frank Hart

Hart reached 128 miles during the first day, soon took the lead, and had a great battle with **Gus Guerrero,** of California, on day three. "Frank Hart is as graceful as of old and came in for his proportion of the liberal applause." Unfortunately, he soon looked haggard. "Frank Hart is virtually out of the race although he occasionally appears upon the track. As he laid prostrate upon his couch last evening, he presented a sad spectacle. His limbs were swollen to nearly twice their natural size, his eyeballs were sunken deeply within their sockets, and the pedal extremities, which had traveled so many miles, were ornamented by large blood blisters. The colored champion will probably never again be seen in a race of this description, as he realizes that the time is at hand when he must acknowledge his younger superiors."

On day five, he was rolling again, but far behind. In the past, he would always quit in these circumstances, but he pressed on. He finished with 425 miles, in sixth place, enough to have a share of the prizes. But because of poor attendance, he did not win much. At least he proved to America that he was not dead yet, and his running career was continuing.

At the end of January 1894, he competed in a 27-hour race in Buffalo, New York, where he finished third with 121 miles but received very little money for his effort. "The dividend for the contestants was hardly perceptible under the microscope." It just wasn't worth it.

Pedestrianism Pauses

Hart and other six-day pedestrians went into serious retirement from competition in 1893. There were only a few six-day races held that year, and Hart did not enter any of them. Some pedestrian historians have written that the sport was a passing fad, that the public had lost interest, or that cycling pushed it aside. This was not entirely true. They failed to understand what truly caused the sport to pause for several years.

This multi-year pause was caused by the panic of 1893 which caused a deep economic depression across America. People rushed to withdraw their money from banks and a credit crunch rippled through the economy. Five hundred banks closed and about 15,000 businesses failed. The unemployment rate was severe in states that had hosted six-day races, 25% in Pennsylvania, 35% in New York, and 43% in Michigan.

The wealthy sports promoters could no longer take the risk of putting on a race that was sure to lose money. Hart again announced his running retirement, but later in 1894 ran a short two-mile race against the legend, Daniel O'Leary and won. The six-day sport took a rest and so did Hart. Because of the depression, from 1893-1897, there were only eight six-day races held in America during those years.

Athletic Trainer in Chicago

In 1895, at the age of 39, Hart started to train again for a 72-hour race he was trying to organize in Chicago, but the race was not held. Since he could not find races to run, he started to go into the athletic training profession and trained bicycle riders with the Aeolus Cycle Club of Chicago.

The early cycling sport was a white-dominant sport, mostly participated by the middle and upper class. The League of American Wheelmen (L.A.W., founded in 1880 in Rhode Island) implemented policies that made it hard for non-whites to enter the sport. Clubhouses were built to store bikes, but they became increasingly exclusionary to the white upper-class males. By 1885, a more affordable bike model was invented in England allowing more women and non-whites to enter the sport. Bike prices fell from $100-150 to about $30. But clubs, including L.A.W. clubs, started to implement more formal bans on memberships. Historian Jesse Gant explained, "Critics were deeply concerned that the bicycle would afford greater mobility and political power. The League thus stepped up its exclusionary efforts after 1893. These labors culminated in a ban on African American bicycling following a League meeting in Louisville, Kentucky, in 1894."

With ultrarunning, Hart had been used to inclusiveness. He could participate in races despite being black. But as he entered the cycling sport in 1895, he saw alarming racist attitudes and he was not shy in speaking out against them. Hart was bold and believed that the same principles seen in ultrarunning/pedestrianism should exist in cycling. He pointed out that in the East, every club had a black trainer, but that was not the case in the West (Midwest).

This quote from Hart revealed his deep feelings about racial barriers and prejudice. "I ride a wheel (bike) and know several other excellent riders of color in the west who have tried to get into the road races but are shut out by that ironclad color exception in the L.A.W. Now if bicycling can be got so that some enterprising manager can put on races and fill them so that every person, regardless of color, can enter them and compete, it will then be truly an American sport. Bicycling as it is now conducted by the L.A.W., is the most narrow and prejudiced of any of the popular sports in the country. All that is needed is a few men with means and who have backbone to make this sport a truly American one. There has always been a color prejudice toward colored men entering any of the sports in this country. I believe that we will yet produce some colored champions in the country, notwithstanding the fact that L.A.W. has forever closed the door on us. The rest of the world is open to us."

In 1896, a devastating landmark ruling was made by the U.S. Supreme Court in the Plessy v. Ferguson case, ruling that racial segregation was legal. Jim Crow laws sprang up and sports segregation laws and rules would make it much harder for future black runners to be fully accepted in the sport. In the years to come, attitudes would reappear that blacks lacked the ability to run long distances and should not compete against whites.

1895 Six-Day Race in Minneapolis, Minnesota

In 1895, Hart still had not retired from six-day racing. In November, he went to Racine, Wisconsin to train for three weeks for a six-day race later in the month in Minneapolis. "He selects Racine on account of the refreshing lake breezes and the seclusion that can be had from outside interference." He trained both on the rural roads and on a tiny indoor horse track at Jerome Case's 200-acre farm. When interviewed by a reporter, he again embellished his career and said very falsely that he had won the Astley Belt in England and was the only black man to be entertained by the Prince of Wales. The city of Racine embraced him, and it was a favorite place for him to visit. "While here, Hart has conducted himself in a gentlemanly manner and has made many friends. He has trained faithfully and is in the pink condition."

	Miles.	Laps.
Glick	458	10
Hart	455	9
Day	455	1
Hegelman	443	7
Taylor	427	0
Campana	420	8
Horan	338	7

The race was held at Washington Avenue Rink, in Minneapolis, on a track fourteen laps to the mile. It was the first six-day race to be held in the city in four years. "The rink has been thoroughly heated, and a profusion of electric lights and bunting make it attractive." It could hold 5,000 spectators and they were entertained by the music of the First Regiment Band. Nineteen runners, including a runner from Cape Town, South Africa, Scotty Kennedy, started. Eight of the runners, including Hart, had experience going over 500 miles in past races. During the first 24 hours, Hart reached 121 miles and he covered 204 miles after 48 hours. In the end, he placed second with 455 miles, but ten miles short of sharing in the gate receipts. For all that effort, he made minimal money.

Giving Back to the Sport

In 1896, Hart continued to live in Chicago, Illinois, and went back to training members of the Aeolus Cycling Club in Chicago with some good success achieved by his riders. While he had no true skill in riding, he was able to teach endurance training and how to succeed in racing for multiple days. He also stayed very busy serving in different roles at race events. He was the chief scorer at a women's six-day bicycle race, and as the judge of walking, at high school and intercollegiate track and field events. He even served as the announcer at a race meet of the Royal Cycling Club in Chicago. He was finally giving back to endurance sports. Some elite cyclists sought out Hart to train them.

Heel-Toe Six-Day Walking Match in St. Louis

At the end of 1896, Hart returned to the Natatorium in St. Louis to complete in a strict heel-toe six-day walking match, 12 hours per day. He assumed command from the start and never lost first place. He won by a few laps with 303 miles. "Hart proved himself to be one of the best things that ever happened in the six-day walking match."

But compared to running, biking, and roller skating, strict heel-toe walking matches were no longer very popular. "The race is too slow and uneventful to suit the populace of today. It is necessary now to satisfy the public taste to travel fast and far, otherwise, the affair ends in the same financial disaster as did the match at the Natatorium. Walking only twelve hours a day did not wear them out so much that they could not recuperate." Spectators wanted to see race contests that involved suffering and crashes.

Bankers Athletic Club

FOR MUSCULAR CHICAGO BANKERS.

Steps Being Taken to Form a Bankers' Athletic Club.

In 1897, Hart, now in his early 40s, was employed as a trainer for the Bankers' Athletic Club in Chicago, Illinois which was established in 1896 for bank clerks, with an initial membership of seven hundred. He trained both runners and cyclists on the south side of Chicago, on the club's grounds on 35th Street with a track, baseball diamond, and grandstands. (It became known as "Banker's Field" and was near the future site of Comisky Park, home of the Chicago White Sox.) They also eventually acquired headquarters for the club at 106 Madison Street on the fifth floor. When Hart was hired, the cycling club had five hundred members. During the summer of 1897, Hart oversaw the outdoor cycling meets organized by the club on their new grounds. He was also employed as the groundkeeper for the baseball diamond. Finally, he had a nice steady job that he enjoyed. At the end of the year, he was appointed secretary of the club.

In February 1898, Hart started personal training for a six-day race to be held during March in Philadelphia, Pennsylvania. "His work consists of running and walking and he is rapidly rounding into shape. He thinks that he is as good a man as he ever was and expressed confidence in his ability to win." It was all for not, the race was canceled.

BANKERS' ATHLETIC IS NO MORE

Association Disbands and Furniture and Fixtures Will Be Sold to Pay Its Debts.

The Bankers' Athletic club folded in late 1898. The lease for their headquarters and gym became too expensive and athletics were abandoned. "Frank Hart, who had been the trainer of the club and had carefully nursed it through its brief career, was the only mourner at the club rooms yesterday. He was made custodian of the club's furniture until it is disposed of at either private or public sale." The reason for closing was because of a lack of interest. "Some members were dissatisfied because no buffet was conducted in the club, others dropped out because the club would not admit to membership others besides bank clerks."

Death of Hart's Wife

On November 19, 1898, Hart's wife, Mary, died at the age of 42 of Tuberculosis, in Boston. He had not lived with her for years. Her address was 56 North Anderson Street, still on the property where they had lived since their marriage. Today a parking garage for Massachusetts General Hospital stands there.

The Last Six-Day Race in Madison Square Garden

In 1899, Hart had hopes to compete in a six-day race to be held in Madison Square Garden, the first there in eight years, but also the last in history. Many "old-time cracks" planned to be there. However, a recent local law limited athletes from contesting for more than 12 hours per day. To get around this law, the event was split into two waves, 12 hours each day, so that it could be a continuous event for six days. Hart was assigned to the second group with many of the old-time famous pedestrians to start at noon.

WALKING MATCH AT AN END.

Pedestrians Quit Work After the Disappearance of the Manager of the Affair.

The whole event illustrated the downfall of the six-day races. From the beginning, it looked like it would be a financial fizzle. Before the second wave finished, the event was canceled because the rent was not paid. The crowds were very small. "**A. R. Samuels**, the manager, looked sadly at the impoverished audience about 10:30 p.m. and had then quietly stepped out to get a breath of fresh air. He did not return. He left behind thirty indignant athletes, some of whom were in bad financial straits, and all of whom had lost sums." Samuels had rented the Garden for $5,000 but took in only $142 on the first day. It appears that Hart quit the failed race very early or wisely did not start. The last six-day race ever held in Madison Square Garden sadly went down in flames. New York City was through with six-day pedestrianism for the next seven decades.

Race Against a Freight Train

In May 1899, Hart started training an amateur runner, **Charles Leroy Buel** (1852-1935), age 36, a sheep salesman, for a stunt. Buel was disgusted with the performance of the Wisconsin Central railroad, which would take 18 hours to transport his sheep from Trevor, Wisconsin, to the Chicago stockyards, about 60 miles. On one trip, some of his sheep died  because of the long, shaky trip. He took up a $500 bet with a railroad man that he could cover the distance on foot faster than the train.

BUEL WINS HIS BET

He Walks from Trevor, Wis., in 13 1-2 Hours, Beating the Wisconsin Central.

DISTANCE 60 MILES

Plucky Sheep Salesman Tires His Pacers and Arrives in Chicago in Good Form.

Buel started on May 20, 1899, at 3:30 a.m., accompanied by Hart as a pacer. "Quite a crowd had gathered at the Trevor depot to witness the departure and cheered as the party disappeared in the darkness." Buel ran eight miles during the first hour, making it difficult for Hart to stay ahead. Two other pacers rode a tandem bike and spelled Hart at times. As Buel entered Chicago, thousands of people lined the sidewalks and cheered him on to the finish. Buel was successful, reaching the stockyards with about five hours to spare, in 13:36. "He stated that he had no intention of being a professional pedestrian, as the stock business was good enough for him."

Hart's Final Six-day Races

Frank Hart's Final Races

Date	City	Place	Miles	Place	Notes
Dec 19-24, 1892	St. Louis, MO	Natatorum	425	6	six-day
Jan 26-27, 1894	Buffalo, NY	Thespian Hall	121		
Nov 25-30, 1895	Minneapolis, MN	Washington Rink	455	2	six-day
Jan 16, 1896	Chicago, IL	Athletic Pavilion	329		28-hour race
Dec 28-Jan 2, 1897	St. Louis, MO	Natatorium	303		
Feb 12-17, 1900	St. Louis, MO	Natatorium	390		
Mar 11-16, 1901	Philadelphia, PA	Industrial Hall	314	8	$90
Apr 15-20, 1901	Columbus, OH	Columbus Auditorium	290	4	12 hours per day
Oct 7-12, 1901	Philadelphia, PA	Industrial Art Hall	207		
Jan 1-5, 1902	St. Louis, MO	West End Coliseum	313	5	97-hour race
Feb 3-8, 1902	Rochester, NY	Fitzhugh Hall	132	DNF	six-day, 8 hours per day
Mar 10-15, 1902	Philadelphia, PA	Industrial Hall	407	7	$100
Mar 31 -Apr 5 1902	Detroit, MI	Light Guard Armory	63	DNF	Quit first day, stomach trouble

On February 11, 1900, Hart, age 43, surprised many when he held a commanding lead in a six-day race held in St. Louis, Missouri. He covered 124 miles during the first 24 hours, and 198 miles in 48

hours, competing with 27 starters. Blisters then plagued him, and he slowed. He finished far down in the standings, with 390 miles.

Hart's Family

With Hart living in Chicago and staying away from Boston for multiple years, where were his children now that his wife was dead? In

Hart's Family in 1900 Census

June 1900, his son **Frank S. Hart** was 23, still living at the North Anderson St home in Boston, with his youngest sister **Adelaide Hart**, age 17, a dressmaker. Also in the home were their aunt and some cousins, relatives of their late mother. Frank Jr. was working as a museum attendant. Two months later he married a white Swedish woman, Ellen Anderson, and he was working as an actor.

On July 30, 1900, Hart married again, to a widow, **Cora (Posey) Thomas** (1858-1924), age 42, from Salt Lake City, Utah. He evidently met her while judging a cycling meet at the Salt Palace saucer track on 9th South between State and Main Street. Cycling promoters had

constructed a unique track with 43-degree banked curves on an oval track, eight laps to a mile. Cyclists from around the country flocked to race on it and try to break world records on the extremely fast track. Hart took some of his trainees there to compete in early July.

Hart and Cora's courtship was fast, just a few weeks. They were married in Grand Rapids, Michigan. In the marriage record, Hart was listed as an athlete, with the West Indies as his birthplace. His parents were listed as Joseph and Elizabeth (Mallory) Hart. Cora was a hairdresser who had been born in Indiana and it was her second marriage. Her first marriage was in 1884 to Samuel Thomas in Indiana. He died in 1897.

Six-Day Races Come Back in Pennsylvania

CROWDS WATCH SIX-DAY WALKERS

Weary "Peds" Cheered on by Three Thousand People Last Night.

A year later, he competed again, this time in Philadelphia, Pennsylvania at the Industrial Hall on Mar 11, 1901. Six-day races had experienced a good resurgence in Pennsylvania. Twenty-four runners started on the 17 laps to a mile track. Still, in great condition, Hart stayed with the leaders and approached 200 miles on day two but suffering from sleep deprivation. "Hart several times staggered against the railing, opened his eyes in surprise, and then plodded sleepily on."

The leader was **John Glick** (1869-1929), a weaver from Germantown, Pennsylvania. He would stagger many times into the wrong hut and started to go cranky. "Music may have charms for the savage beast, but John Glick is not built that way. The sound of the hand organ playing increases his flightiness, and last night he threatened to throw the organ out the window."

Hart struggled on the third day, logging few miles, but was renewed the next day and went around the track "at a lively clip," just hoping to finish well. He was 138 miles behind the leader but still determined and finished in 8th place with 314 miles. He won $90.

Just before the end of the race, Hart kindly wheeled **Peter Hegelman** (1864-1944), a German-American from New York City, around the track on a hand chair to bring attention to him. The doctors would not let Hegelman continue because he was "a little bit gone in his mind." A hat was passed around to collect something for him. Hart came out of this race with a badly sprained ankle with rheumatism.

Peter Hegelman

WHO IS FRANK HART OF BUFFALO?

HE IS ENTERED IN A SIX-DAY RACE NOW ON AT COL-UMBUS. O.

A month later Hart was competing again, this time in Columbus, Ohio. For some reason in the race program, he listed Buffalo, New York, as his hometown. Buffalo was puzzled and asked, "Who is Frank Hart of Buffalo?" Hart again did well, finishing with 290 miles.

In October 1901, he went to compete in Philadelphia and said, "As I have trained thoroughly and conscientiously for this race and I never felt better and strong in my life, I am willing to wager any part of $1,000 that I will cover a greater number of miles than any other named individual in the race." There were 40 starters in the massive race and Hart hung with the leaders. But by day three, he was well down the standings with 207 miles and dropped out the next day.

Training James Dean

In November 1901, Hart took on the responsibility to train/handle James Dean, a stenographer from Boston, Massachusetts. He was another talented black pedestrian who had been beating Hart in recent races. Hart served as Dean's trainer at a six-day race in Pittsburgh's Old City Hall.

RACE HAS LEFT HIM A MANIAC

William Dean, a Pedestrian, Crazed by Week's Awful Grind.

During the race, Dean suddenly accused Hart and his team of attempting to poison him and then would not accept food from them unless it was first tasted by someone to prove that it wasn't poisoned. After he reached 412 miles on the last day of his six-day race, he was in a "daffy" condition, and he was taken to the hospital. He then escaped his attendants while in the bathroom, went through an open window, and down a fire escape.

"A search was at once instituted and kept up for several hours without finding any trace of the missing racer." He was later found wandering the streets and was taken to the police station. "His clothing was covered with blood, the result of a hemorrhage from his nose. He was ragged and covered with dirt. He was wholly irrational and babbled meaninglessly."

St. Francis Hospital

Hart soon arrived and took the "demented man" to St. Francis Hospital. "It is said that Dean was completely broken down from his exertions in the race. He will probably recover after rest and treatment." After another day in the hospital, Dean recovered well and two months later was again competing in a six-day race.

Hart's Last Six-day Race

Hart's last six-day race of his career came March 31, 1902, at Detroit, Michigan, in the Light Guard Armory. It was a great disappointment. He quit on the first day with only 67 miles because of stomach issues. On the next day, the race was stopped because of a lack of funds.

**FIGHT CLOSED
PED'S BENEFIT**

HART AND GOLDEN USED FISTS TO
SETTLE ARGUMENT.

EXHIBITION WAS A FROST, ONLY $24
BEING PAID IN.

PEIER GOLDEN

Later in the week, he participated in short exhibition races on the track to raise funds for runners to return home. Hart controlled how the purses would be dealt out. **Peter Golden** (1943-1933), lodged a protest. "Hot words passed between Golden and Hart, and after the men had prepared themselves for the street, they came together in the armory. They were ordered from the premises and were about to continue the mill on the outside when friends of both men interfered." All this was over only a few dollars. With that, Hart disappeared from competing in the sport at the age of 46. He continued to train athletes.

Hart Seriously Sick

Four years later, in 1906, it was reported that Hart, age 50, was penniless, suffering from tuberculosis, and living in Colorado for his health. Sad news spread across the country that he was dying. He was dependent on friends for all his needs.

Starters of The Great Marathon Race of Missouri

Apparently, Hart was not that low. In May 1906, he was in St. Louis, Missouri, and crewed a runner in "The Great Marathon Race of Missouri" won by the great ultrarunner of the next generation, **Sidney Hatch** (1883-1966) in 2:46:14, just a minute ahead of **Alexander Thibeau**. They were both from Chicago. Hart was crewing for **Lewis Marks** of Chicago, who finished in third place. The runners' crews followed them in automobiles. It was reported, "When Frank Hart, the old negro go-as-you please pedestrian saw Thibeau and Hatch, he jumped out of his auto and, running beside Marks, besought him to run faster. Marks was sore and surly, refused to answer or to run."

Where were the other pedestrians?

In 1906, most of Hart's fellow old-time pedestrians had also retired from the sport, many who also lost their fortunes due to the depression and mismanagement of finances. **Napoleon "Old Sport" Campana** (1836-1906) was selling chewing gum on the streets of Chicago and was seriously ill. **Gus Guerrero** was a gate-tender on the Broadway subway in New York City. **Henry O. Messier** (1862-1945), the sport's historian, was a book salesman. **James Albert** (1856-1912), the American six-day record holder (still holds the record with 621 miles), was operating a cattle ranch in Texas. **Patrick Fitzgerald** (1846-1900), former world record holder and alderman in New York had recently died. The former six-day world record holder, **Robert Vint** (1846-1917), the shoemaker, lived in California. **George D. Noremac** (1852-1922) was operating a hotel in Philadelphia. **Peter Golden** (1943-1933), and **Peter Hegelman** (1864-1944), were clerks in New York City. **John Glick** (1869-1929) was working in the cotton mills in Philadelphia. **Edward C. Moore** (1860-1927) was in Europe working for the Standard Oil company. **Richard Lacouse** (1848-1923) was a bricklayer in Montana. **George W. Guyon** (1853-1933) was a "tinker" in Oklahoma City.

Hart's early trainer, **John D. Oliver "Happy Jack Smith"** (1860-1914) was still training athletes in Massachusetts. Hart's former partner, **Charles A. Harriman** (1853-1919) was a farmer and pastor in Rockport, Maine. Hart's nemesis, **John "Lepper" Hughes** (1850-1921) of New York City, was operating a saloon. Former six-day world record holder from England, **Charles Rowell** (1852-1902) had recently died. Another former world record holder, **Henry "Blower" Brown** (1843-1900) of England had also died. The six-day world record holder, **George Littlewood** (1859-1912) was in business in England. **Daniel O'Leary** (1846-1933), Hart's original mentor, was still walking, and the next year at the age of 61 would conquer the Barclay Match by walking 1,000 miles, one mile each hour, for 1,000 consecutive hours in Cincinnati, Ohio.

Hart's Death

Frank Hart.

On September 17, 1908, Frank Hart died at the age of 52 in his home in Chicago, Illinois due to an attack of pneumonia. "The funeral will be held under the auspices of the lodge of the colored Knights of Pythias, of which he was a member." He was buried under his given name, "Frank E. Hichborn" on September 22, 1908, in Mt. Glenwood Cemetery in Glenwood, Illinois, likely in an unmarked pauper grave. His occupation was listed as "Athletic trainer." Ironically, on his death record, his race was listed as "white." His death, at first, was not widely publicized, only mentioned in Racine, Wisconsin.

Nearly five months later, a detailed article was finally published about his death entitled, "Once Famous, But Died Obscure." "Frank Hart, one of the wonders of the cinder path, died a short time ago in Chicago, with no mention in any paper except that a pauper had passed away and had been buried by charity." It was doubted if his wife and two children who lived in Philadelphia had been notified.

> **Once Famous, But Died Obscure.**
>
> Frank Hart, one of the wonders of the cinder path, died a short time ago in Chicago with no mention in any paper except that a pauper had passed away and had been buried by charity. For years Hart was the world's champion pedestrian. Although known as Hart, his real name was Frank Hichborn, and he was known as such to a great many of the colored people in Chicago and eastern cities. It is nearly six months ago that Hart passed away but it is doubtful if his wife and two children, who live in Philadelphia, have been notified of the fact. H. O. Mess-

others of that class. Hart was a high liver and a good spender. During the last two years he lived on the charity of his friends in Chicago, while his wife and son lived in Philadelphia, and I doubt very much, whether they were aware of his death.

Fellow pedestrian, and trainer of cyclists, **Henry O. Messier,** of Milwaukee, Wisconsin, wrote, "He died penniless in Chicago, and from what I hear, his friends buried him. Hart met and defeated the best six-day go-as-you-please men of the world and won five championship belts. Hart was a high liver and a good spender. During the last two years, he lived on the charity of his friends in Chicago." The *Cleveland Gazette* printed this death announcement with a misprint, stating that Hart had lived on the charity of his friends for 20 years instead of 2 years, which was an error because in those last 20 years Hart received some massive winnings in 50 races and was also a successful trainer. Unfortunately, this error has been copied in many modern pedestrian histories.

Frank Hart's Descendants

Hart did leave behind some posterity, but not many. As he became famous and constantly traveled, he saw less and less of his family. When he died in 1908, he had two living children who likely had no contact with him for years and did not attend his funeral. They were **Frank S. Hart** and **Adelaide Hart Asbury**.

Family Tree

Frank H Hart (1856-1908) – **Mary Augusta Berry** (1855-1898), **Cora Posey** (1856-1924)

Children, grandchildren, great-grandchildren, and great-great-grandchildren

1. **Frank S. Hart** (1876-) – Ellen Anderson (1876-)
2. **Sarah Maynard Hart** (1878-1880)
3. **William Walter Hart** (1880-1880)
4. **Lillian Adelaide Hart** (1881-1881)
5. **Eugenie Adelaide Hart** (1882-1918) – Jasper D. Asbury (1886-1915)
   - **Francis Surry Asbury** (1905-1925)
   - **Howard Augustus deGrasse Asbury** (1907-1978) – Doris T. Wade (1908-1977)
     - **Shirley Evane Asbury** (1926-2011) – Lonnie Lay Jr., Robert Downs
       - **Linda Lay** – Williams
       - **Robert H Downs**
         - **Robert H Downs Jr.** (1979-) – Crystal Franklin
         - **Donese Downs** – Davon Moore
   - **Dorothy Augusta Asbury** (1912-1998) – Daniel Mann (1919-1996)
     - **Donna Maria Mann** (1954-) – Harvey Major, Roberts
       - **Justin Lee Major** (1977-)
   - **George Arthur Asbury** (1913-1993) divorced

Frank's second wife, **Cora (Posey) Hart**, a hairdresser, died in 1924 in Chicago. When Frank died in 1908, it was said that she was living in

Pennsylvania with children. If true, the children were likely from her first marriage.

Son, **Frank S. Hart** was a fast runner in his teens. He married a Swedish white woman, Ellen Anderson. He was an actor and museum attendant at the time, and she was a seamstress who had emigrated to America in 1892.

Daughter, **Eugenie Adelaide "Addie" Hart** was a dressmaker and servant who married a neighbor, Jasper D. G. Asbury. He worked as a porter and later as a lamp repairer. They had four children and always lived in Boston, sometimes with his parents.

Grandson **Howard Asbury** became a dynamic Methodist minister who married Doris Wade. He received a master's degree in theology from Boston University and became an ordained minister in 1939. He was a pastor in Pennsylvania, West Virginia, and New York. From 1943-1954 he was Dean of Religion and head of sociology at Samuel Huston College (black college) and a professor in  the sociology department of Huston-Tillotson College in Austin, Texas. They had one daughter.

 Great-granddaughter **Shirley Evane Ashbury Downs** received a B.A. degree from Clark College in Atlanta in 1947. She taught in the Atlanta public school system and then for most of her career, she worked as a probation officer in New York. She had a daughter, **Linda Lay** (now deceased) by her first marriage. She then married Robert Hartzell Downs. They had a son **Robert H. Downs** and grandchildren, **Robert H. Downs Jr,** of Texas**,** and **Donese Downs Moore** of Georgia. Shirley died in Texas in 2011 at the age of 84. At that time, she had three great-grandchildren.

Grandchild **Dorothy Augusta Asbury** married Daniel Edward Mann. He worked as a porter for American Airlines where he was a "sky cap." They settled in Dorchester, Massachusetts, and had one daughter, in 1954, **Donna Mann Major.**

Great-granddaughter, **Donna Mann** married Harvey L. Major in 1975, had a son **Justin Lee Major**, and later divorced. She has always lived in Massachusetts, and became an MRI technician, working at Brigham and Women's Hospital in Boston. Donna said that in 1997, as part of a mid-life crisis, she took up competitive shooting to do something different. She became the Boston Area Coordinator for the 2nd Amendment Sisters and started hosting ladies shooting events monthly at Boston Gun and Rifle in Dorchester, Massachusetts, along with teaching the Basic Pistol safety class at the club. She founded Boston Urban Action Shooters which hosted indoor shooting matches during the winter months at Mystic Valley Gun Club. Donna was also on the Board of Directors of Commonwealth 2nd Amendment.

Frank Hart's Legacy

Frank Hart was truly one of the greatest American ultrarunners of the 19th century. He made it possible for many black runners of his era to also compete. He was a hero and an idol. Running was certainly his entire life, but he had his serious flaws. His drive for fame and fortune came at the expense of his family and many friends who tried to help him but were pushed away. He was determined to excel and sought the recognition he deserved, but often was not given enough respect because he was black.

Hart competed in at least 113 ultras during his career that spanned 1879-1902, 23 years. He reached 100 miles in about 80 races. In most of those races, he went much further than 100 miles. The six-day race was his favorite event and he participated in at least 64 six-day races during his lifetime. He totaled at least 26,000 miles during his races and probably had five times those miles in training.

While most Americans have never heard of Frank Hart before, he remains one of the first nationally famous black athletes in America, the Jackie Robison of 19th-century ultrarunning/pedestrianism. Sadly, as Jim Crow laws and more bigotry took hold in the 20th century, all sports experienced a setback in inclusiveness. There were some exceptions. In 1928, **Charles C. Pyle** (1882-1939) allowed five black ultrarunners to compete in his race across America, nicknamed, "The Bunion Derby." It wasn't until the 1950s that **Ted Corbitt** (1919-2007) of New York City, again crossed that racial barrier and became the "Father of American Long-Distance Running" in the modern era. But Frank Hart was truly the first black famous ultrarunner in history.

Frank Hart's Career Races

Frank Hart's Career Races

	Date	City	Place	Miles	Place	Notes
1	Apr 25-26, 1879	Boston, MA	Music Hall	119	1	30 hour. $100
2	May 14, 1879	Lowell, MA	Huntington Hall	50	1	50-miler 8:50
3	May 21, 1879	Boston, MA	Mammoth Tent	39	2	Beanpot, $45
4	May 26-31, 1879	Boston, MA	Mammoth Tent	424	1	six-day, Interstate, $150
5	Jul 23-26, 1879	Boston, MA	Music Hall	263	2	75-hour 3 day, $150
6	Sep 8-13, 1879	Providence, RI	Park Garden	363	1	six-day, Champion Belt, $300
7	Sep 22-28, 1879	New York City, NY	Madison Square Garden	450	4	six-day, 5th Astley Belt, $3,750
8	Oct 22, 1879	Long Island, NY	Frunell's Athletic Park	61	3	12 hour race, $12.60
9	Nov 24-29, 1879	Newark, NJ	Newark Rink	373	1	six-day, 12 hours per day, $500
10	Dec 22-27, 1879	New York City	Madison Square Garden	540	1	six-day, Rose Belt, $3,000
11	Apr 5-10, 1880	New York City	Madison Square Garden	565	1	six-day, 2nd O'Leary Belt, WR, $21,567
12	Feb 28-Mar 5, 1881	New York City	Madison Square Garden	63	DNF	six-day, 3rd O'Leary Belt, quit 1st day
13	Dec 7-10, 1881	Memphis, TN	Exposition Building	306	1	75 Hours
14	Dec 26-31, 1881	New York City	American Institute	229	DNF	six-day, quit on 3rd day
15	Feb 27-Mar 4, 1882	New York City	Madison Square Garden	542	4	six-day, Diamond Whip, $1,500
16	Apr 11-14, 1882	Nashville, TN	Rink	268	1	100-hour race
17	Apr 24-29, 1882	Memphis, TN	Exposition Building	425	1	123-hour race
18	May 12-15, 1882	Little Rock, AR	Alexander Park Hall		DNF	Four-day race
19	Jun 23-24, 1882	Springfield, MA	The Rink	127	2	26-hour race
20	Jul 31-Aug 5, 1882	Boston, MA	Casino to Five	527	1	six-day, Police Gazette Diamond Belt
21	Oct 23-29, 1882	New York City	Madison Square Garden	482	5	six-day, World Championship
22	Mar 17, 1883	Troy, New York	Hall	121		26-hour race
23	May 28-Jun 2, 1883	Baltimore, MD	Kernan's Monumental Th	400	4	six-day, Fox Diamond Belt
24	Jun 27-29, 1883	Fall River, MA	Forest Hill Gardens			5 hours each night
25	Sep 10-15, 1883	Baltimore, MD	Kernan's Monumental Th	417	1	
26	Oct 19, 1883	Holyoke, MA	Front Street Rink	35	DNF	with women
27	Nov 21-26, 1883	San Francisco, CA	Mechanics's Pavilion	500	1	six day, Pacific Slope Championship
28	Jan 14-19, 1884	San Francisco, CA	Mechanics's Pavilion	487	1	Muldoon's Great Six Days Race
29	Mar 12, 1884	Los Angeles, CA	Turn Verein Hall	25	1	25-mile walking exhibition, 8:27:30
30	May 19-24, 1884	Denver, CO	Belmont & Hanson's Rin	416	2	match against Edward Williams
31	Jul 7-12, 1884	Chicago, IL	Battery D Armory	58	DNF	DNF in protest over scoring
32	Jun 8-13, 1885	Baltimore, MD	Kernan's Monumental Theatre		DNF	quit on 4th day
33	Aug 1885	Paterson, NJ	Little Coney Island Cours	48		50-mile walking record attempt
34	Aug 17-22, 1885	Paterson, NJ	Little Coney Island Course			
35	Oct 5-10, 1885	Binghamton, NY		207		75 hours race
36	Oct 28-31, 1885	Scranton, PA	Lackawanna Rink	234	4	75 hours race
37	Feb 10-12, 1886	Williamsport, PA	Keystone Rink	251	2	75 hour race
38	Mar 1-5, 1886	Cincinnati, OH	Queen City Rink			six-day
39	Mar 22-25, 1886	York, PA	York Skating Rink			match against Harriman
40	Apr 8-9, 1886	Scranton, PA	Arcadian Rink			51-hour race
41	Apr 16-17, 1886	Bradford, PA	Parlor Rink	265	1	75 hour race
42	Apr 26-27, 1886	Carbondale, PA	Metropolitan Rink	183	1	51-hour race
43	Aug 2-7, 1886	Paterson, NJ	Little Coney Island	>319	1	12 hours per day
44	Oct 4-9, 1886	New Bedford, MA	Bandcroft Rink	280	DNF	quit on day five
45	Oct 21-23, 1886	Pittston, PA	West Pittston Rink	136+		75-hour race
46	Nov 1-5, 1886	Boston, MA	Columbia Rink	205		six day, 12 hours per day
47	Jan 5-9, 1887	Utica, NY	Lafayette Rink	245	3	heel-toe
48	Feb 20-25, 1887	Philadelphia, PA	Elite Rink	518	2	six-day, $2,000
49	Mar 14-15, 1887	Jackson, MI	Assembly Opera House	>96		50-hour match
50	Apr 2, 1887	Jackson, MI	Assembly Opera House	15	1	15-mile walking match, 2:22:26
51	May 2-7, 1887	Philadelphia, PA	Elite Rink	485	4	six-day
52	May 18-21, 1887	Lincoln, NE	Funke's Opera House	199	2	50-hour race
53	Jun 6-11, 1887	Omaha, NE	Exposistion Building	400	1	six days
54	Sep 19-24, 1887	Oshkosh, WI	Casino Rink			Duel match with Harriman

Frank Hart's Career Races

	Date	City	Place	Miles	Place	Notes
55	Oct 10-15, 1887	Philadelphia, PA	Columbia Rink	376	1	six day, 12 hours per day
56	Oct 19-21, 1887	New Bedford, MA	Adelphi Rink			75-hour race
57	Nov 21-26, 1887	Philadelphia, PA	Elite Rink	118	DNF	quit on day two
58	Dec 26-31, 1887	Kansas City, MO		429	2	six-day
59	Feb 6-11, 1888	New York City, NY	Madison Square Garden	546	4	six-days, $2,500
60	Mar 9-10, 1888	Birmingham, CT	Tingue Rink		DNF	DNF
61	Mar 30-21, 1888	Fair Haven, CT	Quinnipiac Rink	>100	1	won, $75
62	Apr 9-14, 1888	Denver, CO	Mammoth Rink	473	1	six-day
63	May 7-12, 1888	New York City, NY	Madison Square Garden	122	DNF	six, days, quit day two
64	May 19, 1888	New York City, NY	Recreation Hall	124	2	24-hour race
65	Jun 1-2, 1888	Ansonia, CT		134	1	27-hour race
66	Aug 9-11, 1888	Troy, New York		292	1	75 hour race
67	Oct 3-6, 1888	Willmington, DE	Wilmington Rink	216	1	75 hour race, $160
68	Oct 18-20, 1888	Philadelphia, PA	Elite Rink	279	1	$80
69	Nov 26-Dec 1, 1888	New York City	Madison Square Garden	539	6	six-day. $463, Littlewood WR
70	Dec 24-29, 1888	Pittsburgh, PA	London Theater	86		
71	Jan 10-12, 1889	Fair Haven, CT	Quinnipiac Rink		DNF	50-hour race, DNF
72	Jan 30-Feb 1, 1889	Bangor, ME	Norombega Hall	104	3	27-hour race, 20 laps to a mile, $25
73	Feb 22-17, 1889	San Francisco, CA	Mechanics' Pavilion	525	1	six-day, $3,720
74	Mar 21-23, 1889	San Jose, CA	Horticultural Hall	148	2	32-hour match, 8 hours per day
75	May 10-15, 1889	San Francisco, CA	Mechanics' Pavilion	203	DNF	Quit on third day
76	Jun 12-15, 1889	Santa Cruz, CA	Pavilion	180	2	four days, four hours per day
77	Oct 21-26, 1889	Tacoma, WA	Alpha Opera House	150	2	four days, four hours per day
78	Nov 9, 1889	Victoria, BC		10		ten mile mach against Ed Shade
79	Dec 23-28, 1889	Cleveland, OH		>131		
80	Jan 1, 1890	Pittsburgh, PA	London Theater	11	DNF	12 hour exhibition, quit very early
81	Feb 24-Mar 1, 1890	Detroit, MI	Detroit Rink	106	DNF	Quit on day two
82	Apr 7-12, 1890	Pittsburgh, PA	Grand Central Rink	77	DNF	Quit on day one
83	May 21-24, 1890	Chicago, IL	Second Regiment Armory		DNF	75-hour race, quit on day one
84	Sep 2-7, 1890	Detroit, MI	Detroit Rink	479	1	six-day, $780
85	Oct 15-18, 1890	Altoona, PA	Emerald Hall	258	3	72-hour race
86	Jan 26-Jan 31, 1891	Minneapolis, MN	Washington Rink	186	DNF	quit day four, swollen knee
87	Feb 24-Mar 1, 1891	St. Paul, MN	Lowry Arcade	378	2	six-day, 12 hours per day, $370
88	Mar 16-21-1891	New York City	Madison Square Garden	100	DNF	Quit after day one
89	Apr 15-18, 1891	Boston, MA	Winslow's Rink	68	DNF	Quit on the first day
90	May 15-20, 1891	St. Paul, MN	Mussetter's Drug Store	244	DNF	1,000 mile race, ten hours per day
91	Jun 8-13, 1891	Denver, CO	Coliseum Hall	>100	DNF	Cancelled early for poor attendance
92	Aug 10-19, 1891	Minneapolis, MN	Shade's Park	94	6	six-day, four hours per day
93	Sep 29-Oct 4, 1891	Elmira, NY	Madison Ave Square	238		
94	Dec 21-26, 1891	St. Louis, MO	Natatorium	280	DNF	Quit day four, blisters
95	Jan 13-18, 1892	Kansas City, MO	Vineyard's Hall	132	DNF	12.5 hours per day, quit on day three
96	Feb 22-27, 1892	New Orleans, LA	Washington Artillery Hal	215	DNF	Quit on day four, out of the money
97	Apr 25-30, 1892	Minneapolis, MN	Panorama Building	310	2	12 hours per day, $250
98	May 17-22, 1892	St. Paul, MN	Jackson St. Rink		3	12 hours per day
99	Oct 17-22, 1892	Chicago, IL	Second Regiment Armor	479	1	five-day
100	Nov 21-25, 1892	Racine, WI	Belle City Hall	62	DNF	six day, four hours per day, blood
101	Dec 19-24, 1892	St. Louis, MO	Natatorium	425	6	six-day
102	Jan 26-27, 1894	Buffalo, NY	Thespian Hall	121		
103	Nov 25-30, 1895	Minneapolis, MN	Washington Rink	455	2	six-day
104	Jan 16, 1896	Chicago, IL	Athletic Pavilion	329		28-hour race
105	Dec 28-Jan 2, 1897	St. Louis, MO	Natatorium	303		
106	Feb 12-17, 1900	St. Louis, MO	Natatorium	390		
107	Mar 11-16, 1901	Philadelphia, PA	Industrial Hall	314	8	$90
108	Apr 15-20, 1901	Columbus, OH	Columbus Auditorium	290	4	12 hours per day
109	Oct 7-12, 1901	Philadelphia, PA	Industrial Art Hall	207		
110	Jan 1-5, 1902	St. Louis, MO	West End Coliseum	313	5	97-hour race
111	Feb 3-8, 1902	Rochester, NY	Fitzhugh Hall	132	DNF	six-day, 8 hours per day
112	Mar 10-15, 1902	Philadelphia, PA	Industrial Hall	407	7	$100
113	Mar 31 -Apr 5 1902	Detroit, MI	Light Guard Armory	63	DNF	Quit first day, stomach trouble

Sources

Chapter 1 Sources

- P.S. Marshall, *King of the Peds*
- Ancestry.com: marriage, birth, and death records. Census records.
- National Republican (Washington D.C.) Apr 17, 1876
- The Boston Globe (Massachusetts), Apr 13, 25-27, Sep 3, 10, 17, 22-23, 29-30, 1879
- The Fitchburg Sentinel (Massachusetts), May 31, 1879
- New York Daily Herald (New York), Aug 29, Sep 23-28, 1879
- The Times-Picayune (New Orleans), Sep 2, 1879
- The Philadelphia Inquirer (Pennsylvania), Sep 9, 1879
- The Baltimore Sun (Maryland), Sep 15, 1879
- The Buffalo Commercial (New York), Sep 22, 1879
- The New York Times (New York), Sep 22, 1879
- The Brooklyn Daily Eagle (New York), Sep 23, 28, 1879
- The Sun (New York), Sep 23, 1879
- Chicago Daily Telegraph (Illinois), Sep 23, 1879
- Buffalo Courier (New York), Sep 28, 1879
- Boston Post (Massachusetts), Sep 29, 1879
- Reading Times (Pennsylvania), Sep 22, 29, 1879
- Daily Republican (Wilmington, Delaware), Oct 7, 1879

Chapter 2 Sources

- P.S. Marshall, *King of the Peds*
- Ancestry.com: marriage, birth, and death records. Census records.
- Tom Osler and Ed Dodd, *Ultra-Marathoning: The Next Challenge*
- The Boston Globe (Massachusetts), Oct 14-15, 23, Dec 17, 1879, Jan 3-4, 6, 28, Feb 5, Mar 10, Apr 7, 11-12, 24, Jul 25, 27, 28, Aug 6, 8, 22, Sep 26, Oct 3-4, 17, 21, Nov 8, Dec 19, 1880, Jan 9, 1881, Dec 19, 24, Nov 27, 1914
- The Inter Ocean (Chicago, Illinois), Oct 11, 1879
- The New York Times (New York), Dec 23-27, 1879, Mar 28, Apr 11, 1880
- The Sun (New York, New York), Dec 26 28, 1879, Apr 6-11, Dec 29, 1880
- New York Daily Herald (New York), Dec 29, 1879

- The Buffalo Commercial (New York), Dec 30, 1879
- The Brooklyn Daily Eagle (New York), Dec 23, 1879, Apr 9-12, 1880
- The Sacramento Bee (California), Apr 1, 1880
- The Fall River Daily Herald (Massachusetts), Apr 5, 1880
- The Times-Picayune (Louisiana, New Orleans), Apr 12, 1880
- St. Louis Post-Dispatch (Missouri), Apr 12, 1880
- The South Bend Tribune (Indiana), Apr 12, 1880
- The Comet (Jackson, Mississippi), Oct 4, 1879, Apr 14, 1880
- Knoxville Whig and Chronicle (Tennessee), Apr 21, 1880
- The Greeley Tribune (Kansas), Apr 30, 1880
- The Western Spirit (Paola, Kansas), Apr 30, 1880
- Evening Mail (London, England), Apr 28, 1880
- Buffalo Morning Express (New York), Jul 27, Aug 18, 1880
- The Baltimore Sun (Maryland), Jul 30, 1880
- The Ottawa Free Trader (Canada), Aug 14, 1880
- The San Francisco Examiner (California), Aug 20-21, 1933

Chapter 3 Sources

- P.S. Marshall, *King of the Peds*
- Ancestry.com: marriage, birth, and death records. Census records.
- Buffalo Morning Express (New York), Apr 24, 1878
- The Boston Globe (Massachusetts), Jan 31, Feb 23, Mar 3, Jun 5, Jul 5, 10, Aug 10, Dec 30, 1881, Jan 22, Feb 19, 24, 26-28, Mar 1-5, 26, Apr 22, Jun 25, Aug 1-6, 13, Oct 4, 23, 28, 1882
- The Buffalo Commercial (New York), Jan 10, Apr 21, 1881, Feb 18, 1882
- The Brooklyn Union (New York), Feb 21, Jun 4, 1881, Jun 1, 1883
- The Sun (New York, New York), Feb 22-23, 28, Mar 1, Dec 26, 28, 1881, Mar 5, Oct 27-28, 1882, Mar 18, 1883
- New York Tribune (New York), Feb 28, Mar 1, 1881
- Louis Globe-Democrat (Missouri), Apr 19, 1881
- The San Francisco Examiner (California), May 9, 1881
- The Weekly Dispatch (London, England), Jun 12, 1881
- Edinburgh Evening News (Scotland), Jun 6, 1881
- San Francisco Chronicle (California), Jun 16, 1881, Feb 14, 1889
- The Fall River Daily Herald (Massachusetts), Oct 3, 1881
- Chicago Tribune (Illinois), Nov 27, 1881, Mar 19, 1883

- The Daily Memphis Avalanche (Tennessee), Dec 8, 1881
- Buffalo Morning Express (New York), Dec 29, 1881
- The New York Times (New York), Dec 29, 1881, Feb 27, Mar 9, 1882
- Kansas City Times (Missouri), Feb 16, 1882
- The Times Leader (Wilkes-Barre, Pennsylvania), Mar 10, 1882
- The Tennessean (Nashville, Tennessee), Apr 11, 1882
- Boston Evening Transcript (Massachusetts), Jun 15, 1882
- The Fall River Daily Herald (Massachusetts), Jun 26, Dec 4, 1882
- The Cincinnati Enquirer (Ohio), Aug 1, Oct 3, 1882
- The Brooklyn Daily Eagle (New York), Oct 23, 1882
- The Critic (Washington D.C.), Jun 1, 1883

Chapter 4 Sources

- P.S. Marshall, *King of the Peds*
- Matthew Algeo, *Pedestrianism: When Watching People Walk Was American's Favorite Spectator Sport*
- The Boston Globe (Massachusetts), Dec 31, 1882, Sep 10-11, Nov 8, 20, 1883, Jul 16, 1884, Mar 1-10, 15, 17, Apr 10, 13, 16, May 8, Aug 10, Nov 28, 1885, Oct 9, 14, Nov 9, 28, 1886, Feb 12, 1888
- The San Francisco Examiner (California), Nov 8, 11, 15, 18, 22-25, Dec 4, 1883, Jan 3, 7, 11-20, Feb 21, 23, Mar 24, Jul 7, 1884
- The Record Union (Sacramento, California), Nov 17, 1883, Feb 11, 1884
- San Francisco Chronicle (California), Jan 20, 1884
- The Fall River Daily Herald (Massachusetts), Mar 24, 1884
- The Sun (New York, New York), Apr 23, 1884, Feb 12, 1888
- The New York Times (New York), Apr 28, 1884
- The Evening Telegraph (Buffalo, New York), May 3, 1884
- Louis Post-Dispatch (Missouri) Jun 4, 1884
- Brooklyn Times Union (New York), May 22, 1884
- The Butte Miner (Montana), May 25, 1884
- The Inter Ocean (Chicago, Illinois), Jul 8, 1884, Apr 3, 1887
- Chicago Tribune (Illinois), Jul 13, 1884
- The Cincinnati Enquirer (Ohio), Aug 15, 1884
- Detroit Free Press (Michigan), Sep 27, 1884
- Memphis Daily Appeal (Tennessee), Dec 7, 26, 1884
- The Gazette (Montreal, Canada), Aug 11, 1885
- The Brooklyn Daily Eagle (New York), Aug 14, 1885

- Evening Star (Washington, D.C.) Oct 16, 1885
- The Democratic Age (York, Pennsylvania), Mar 23, 1886
- Buffalo Courier (New York), Apr 18, 1886, May 23, 1887
- The Brooklyn Citizen (New York), Jan 16, 1887
- Halifax Herald (Nova Scotia, Canada), Jan 22, 1887
- The Philadelphia Inquirer (Pennsylvania), Feb 21-27, May 2-7, 1887
- The Philadelphia Times (Pennsylvania), Feb 21-27, May 2-7, 1887
- Sunday News (Wilkes-Barre, Pennsylvania), May 8, 1887
- The Oshkosh Northwestern (Wisconsin), Sep 27, 1887
- The Evening World (New York, New York), Feb 6-11, 1888
- The Morning Call (Paterson, New Jersey), Feb 12, 1888

Chapter 5 Sources

- The Meriden Daily Journal (Connecticut), Apr 2, 1888
- The Santa Fe New Mexican (New Mexico), Apr 19, 1888
- New York Times (New York), May 6, 1888
- The Evening World (New York, New York), May 7, Nov 23, 27-30, 1888, Feb 6, 1889
- The Waterbury Democrat (Connecticut), Jun 4, 1889
- The Brooklyn Citizen (New York), Nov 26, 1888, Mar 1, 1891
- The Kansas City Star (Missouri), Nov 30, 1888
- The Boston Globe (Massachusetts), Dec 2, 1888, Apr 14, 1891
- Lancaster Daily Intelligencer (Pennsylvania), Feb 7, 1889
- The San Francisco Examiner (California), Feb 22-28, Mar 1, 11, Apr 28, May 10-16, 1889
- San Francisco Chronicle (California), Feb 28, May 14, 16, 1889
- The Los Angeles Times (California), Oct 27, 1889
- Pittsburgh Post-Gazette (Pennsylvania), Dec 18, 1889
- Pittsburgh Dispatch (Pennsylvania), Feb 16, Mar 28, 1890
- Pittsburgh Press (Pennsylvania), Apr 7, 1890
- Detroit Free Press (Michigan), Sep 2-8, 1890
- Altoona Times (Pennsylvania), Oct 15-20, 1890
- The St. Paul Globe (Minnesota), Mar 2, 1891, May 7, 1891, May 22, 1892
- The Brooklyn Daily Eagle (New York), Mar 9, 1891
- La Plata Home Press (Missouri), May 29, 1891
- Star Tribune (Minneapolis, Minnesota), May 15, 1891
- Star-Gazette (Elmira, New York), Oct 2-3, 1891

- Louis Post-Dispatch (Missouri), Dec 13, 22, 1891, Dec 3, 21-26 1892, May 28, 1895
- The Kansas City Times (Missouri), Jan 15, 1892
- The Times-Democrat (New Orleans, Louisiana), Feb 26, 1892
- The Times-Picayune (New Orleans, Louisiana), Feb 25, 1892
- The Inter Ocean (Chicago, Illinois), Oct 18-19, 1892, Aug 4, 1894
- Journal Times (Racine, Wisconsin), Nov 25, 1892

Chapter 6 Sources

- Ancestry.com: marriage, birth, and death records. Census records.
- St. Louis Globe-Democrat (Missouri), Dec 13, 20, 1892, Jan 4, 1897, Feb 12-18, 1900
- St. Louis Post-Dispatch (Missouri), Dec 13, 23, 1892, May 6, 1906
- Pittsburgh Post-Gazette (Pennsylvania), Dec 17, 1892
- Vancouver Daily World (British Columbia, Canada), Dec 22, 1892
- Manitoba Semi-Weekly Free Press (Winnipeg, Canada), Dec 26, 1892
- Chicago Tribune (Illinois), Jan 23, 1897, Nov 18, 1898
- The Inter Ocean (Chicago, Illinois), Aug 4, 1894, Feb 1, 1898
- Buffalo Courier (New York), Jan 28, 1894
- Jesse Gant, 19th Century, 20th Century Whites on Bikes
- Molly Huber, Bicycling Craze, 1890s
- The Boston Globe (Massachusetts), Nov 28, 1892, Aug 7, 1895, Mar 13, 2005
- The Journal Times (Racine, Wisconsin), Nov 15, 27, 1895
- The Saint Paul Globe (Minnesota), Nov 24, 1895
- Star Tribune (Minneapolis, Minnesota), Dec 1, 1895
- The Chicago Chronicle (Illinois), Apr 26, 1896
- The Nashville American (Tennessee), Jan 23, 1899
- The Brooklyn Citizen (New York), Jun 11, 1899
- The Salt Lake Tribune (Utah), Jun 8, 1900
- Philadelphia Times (Pennsylvania), Mar 9, 13, 16, Apr 16, 1901, Mar 16-17, 1902
- Philadelphia Inquirer (Pennsylvania), Mar 14-18, 1901
- The Buffalo Times (New York), Apr 16, 1901
- The Wilkes-Barre Record (Pennsylvania), Oct 10, 1901
- The Pittsburgh Press (Pennsylvania), Nov 17, 1901
- The New York Times (New York), Feb 8, 1902
- Detroit Free Press (Michigan), Apr 6, 1902

- Post-Crescent (Appleton, Wisconsin), Feb 28, 1906
- The Post-Crescent (Appleton, Wisconsin), Feb 28, 1906
- The Journal Times (Racine, Wisconsin), Sep 23, 1908
- The Kansas City Star (Missouri), Feb 7, 1909
- The Lincon Star (Kansas), Feb 9, 1909

About the Author

David "Davy" R. Crockett is a veteran ultrarunner and historian. He began serious running in 2004 and finished more than one hundred 100-mile races during the next fourteen years. In 2005, he combined his love for running and history by organizing the "Pony Express Trail 50 and 100" held on the historic Pony Express Trail in the west desert of Utah.

In 2016, he developed an interest in the history of ultrarunning, and the true origins of the 100-mile race. He soon uncovered the bomb-shell discovery about the true first finishers of Western States 100 in 1972, shattering the race origin story claims made by the race for decades.

In 2018, he established ultrarunninghistory.com and the Ultrarunning History Podcast, authoring long articles and episodes every two weeks documenting long-forgotten stories of the sport.

In 2020, he became the new Director of the American Ultrarunning Hall of Fame which is hosted on ultrarunninghistory.com

In 2021, after the International Association of Ultrarunning (IAU) announced plans to no longer recognize six-day races, the very race that historically began ultrarunning/pedestrianism in the 19th century, he took on the task to inform the sport of the rich six-day race history that was being forgotten. In the process of compiling the history, he decided that a book deserved to be written about Frank Hart, one of the great pioneers of the sport.

Davy Crockett is the author of four previous books on the American 19th-century westward migration. He has published numerous articles in magazines and newspapers. In addition, he has previously written two free online books on ultrarunning, including his running memoir, *My Path to Ultrarunning.*

He and his wife Linda are the parents of six children and eleven grandchildren, all living in Utah.

Ultrarunninghistory.com

Crockettclan.org/blog

Acknowledgments

Thanks to **Andy Milroy** of England for inspiring and guiding me in my quest to learn and understand the history of ultrarunning. Thanks to **P.S. Marshall** for his exhaustive collection of early pedestrianism and outstanding reference book, "King of the Peds. Thanks to ultrarunning legendary **Ed Dodd** for reintroducing the American ultrarunning sport to pedestrianism history in 1979 and was instrumental in bringing back the six-day race after more than 70 years of absence. Thanks to my dedicated audience of Ultrarunning History Podcast, who have encouraged me to start collecting my writings into books so they can be preserved.

Listen to the Ultrarunning History Podcast in your favorite podcast app or on ultrarunninghistory.com. You can also watch the episodes on the Ultrarunning History YouTube Channel.

Index of Names

Printed in Great Britain
by Amazon

13793656R00078